DOG

AND DOODLE DESIGNS

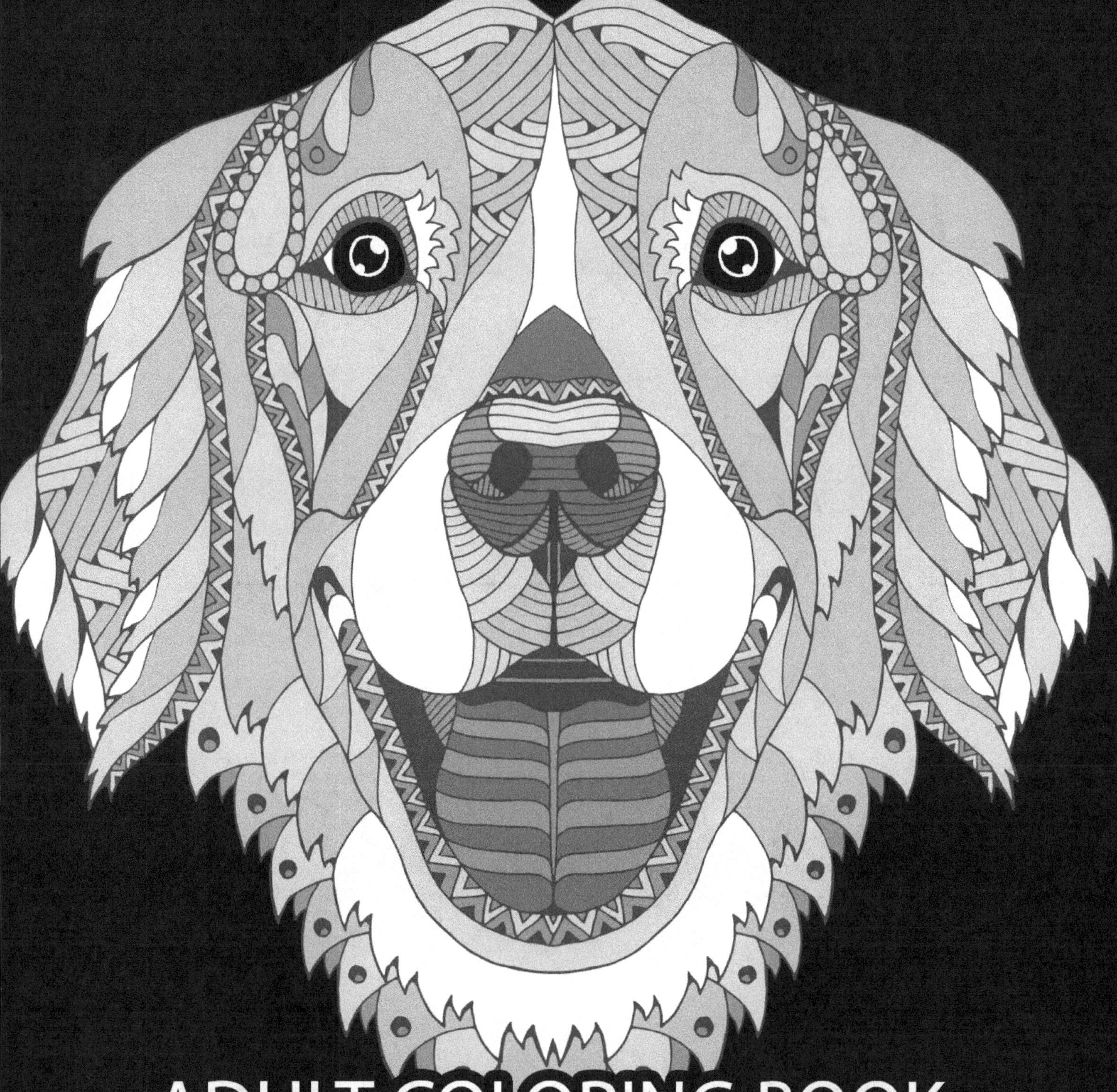

ADULT COLORING BOOK

TEST YOUR COLOR

TEST YOUR COLOR

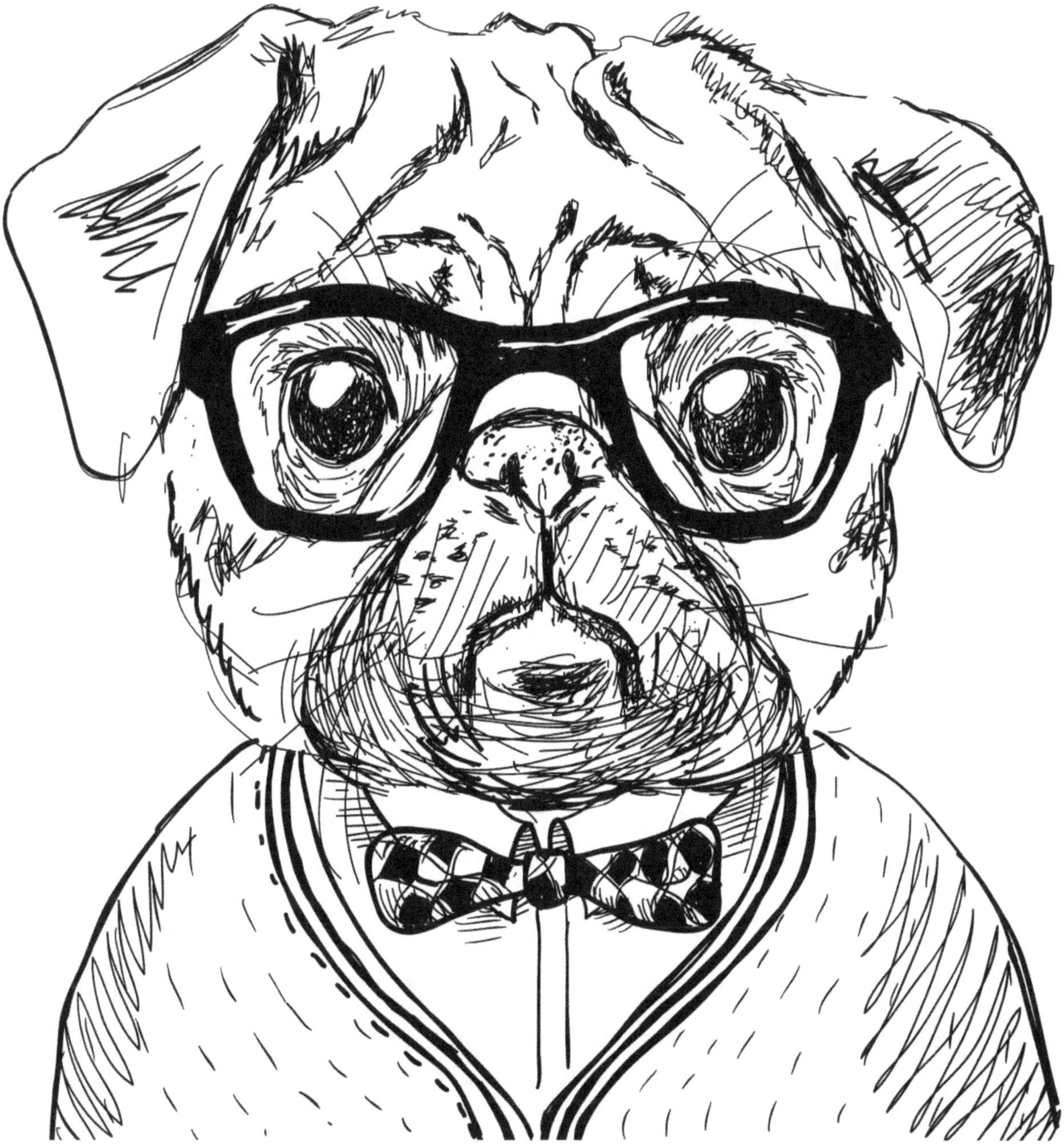

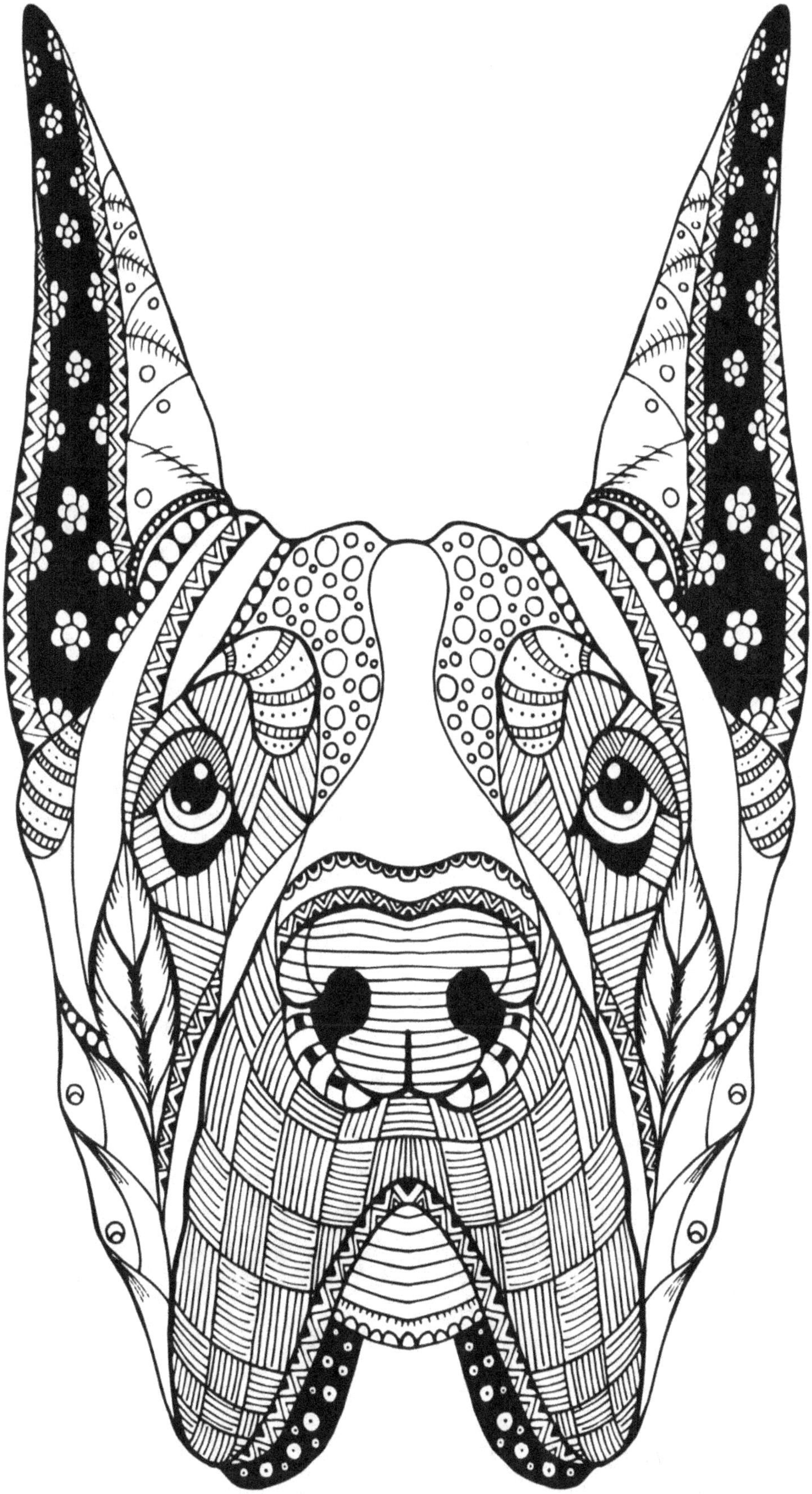

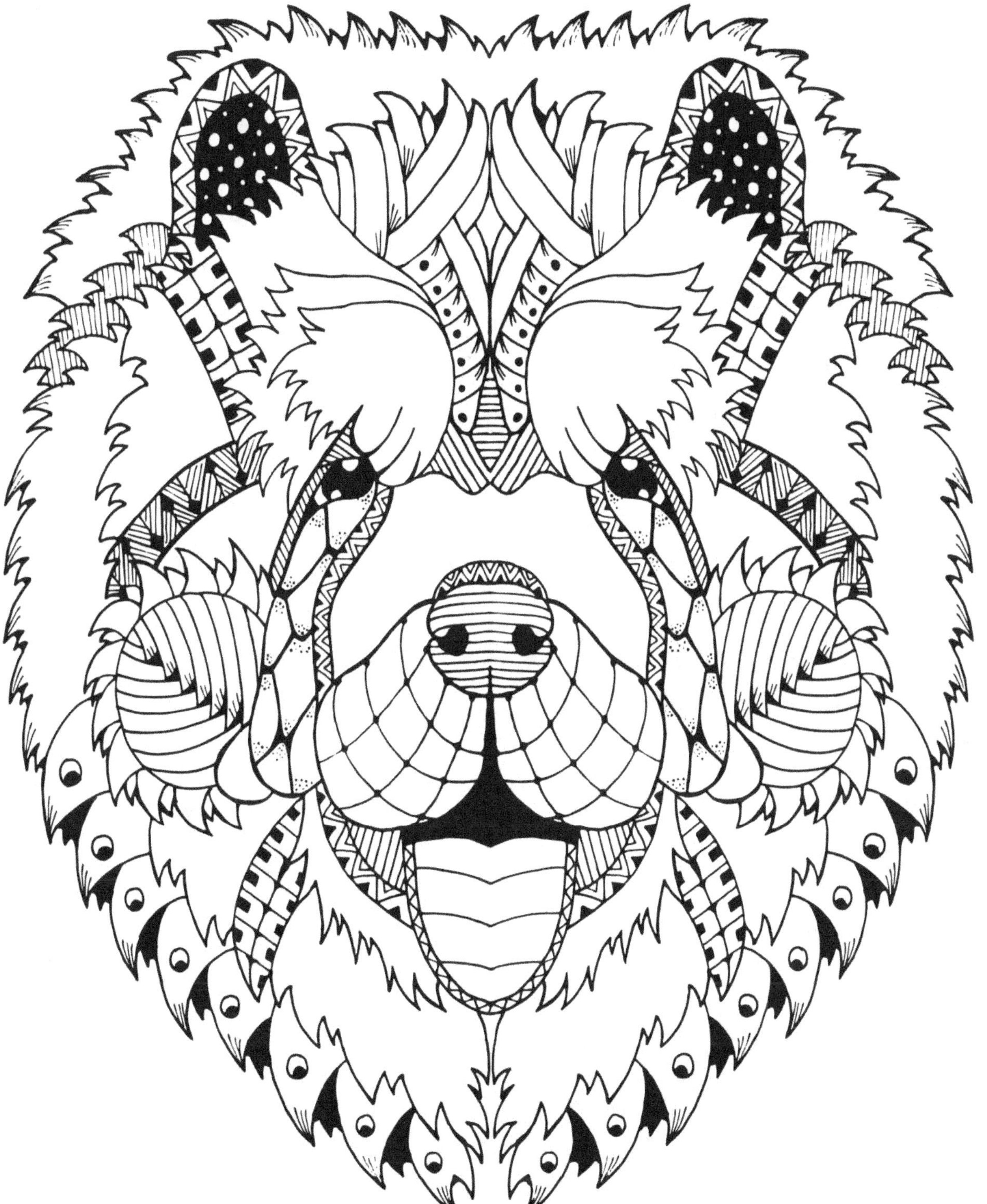

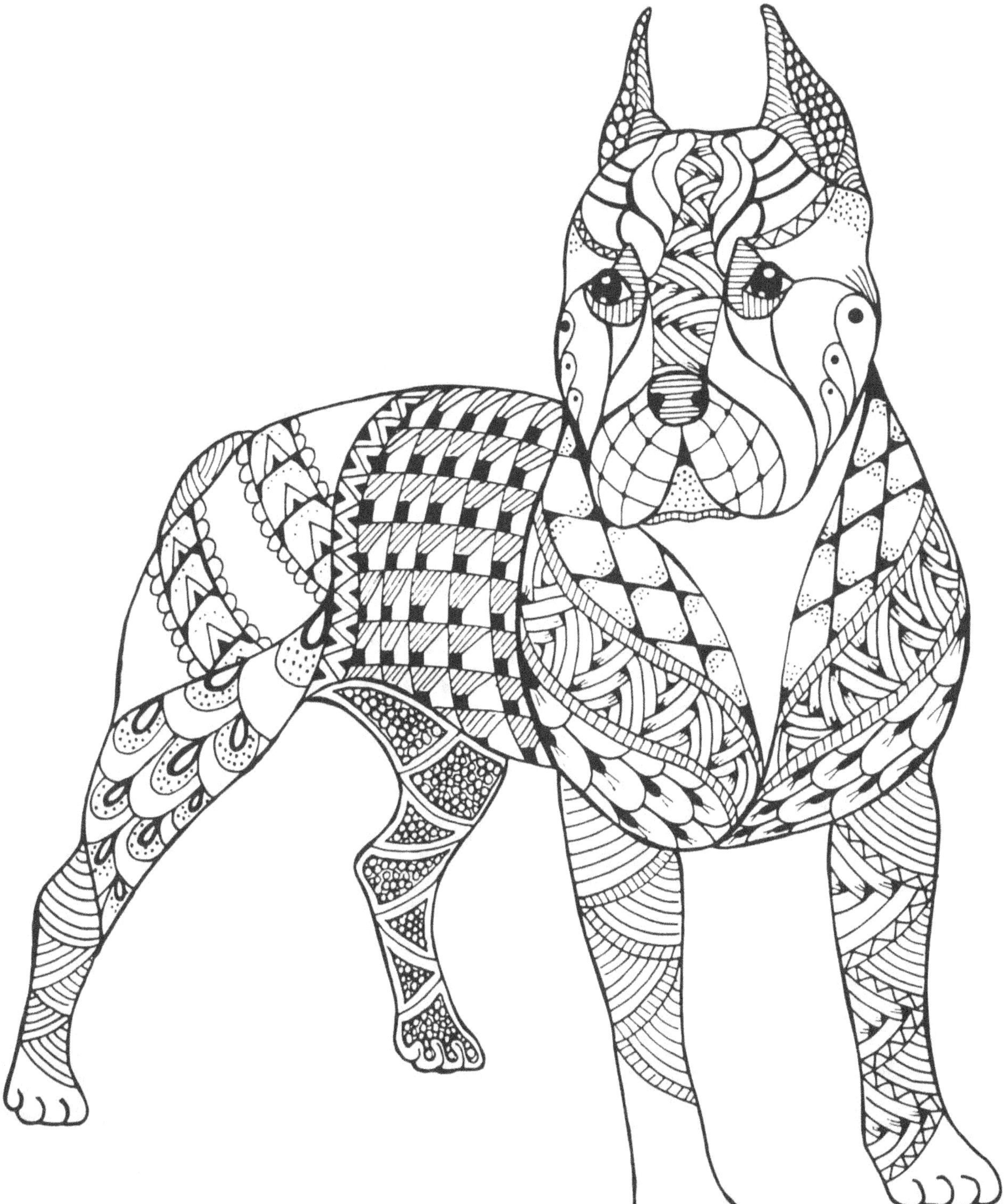

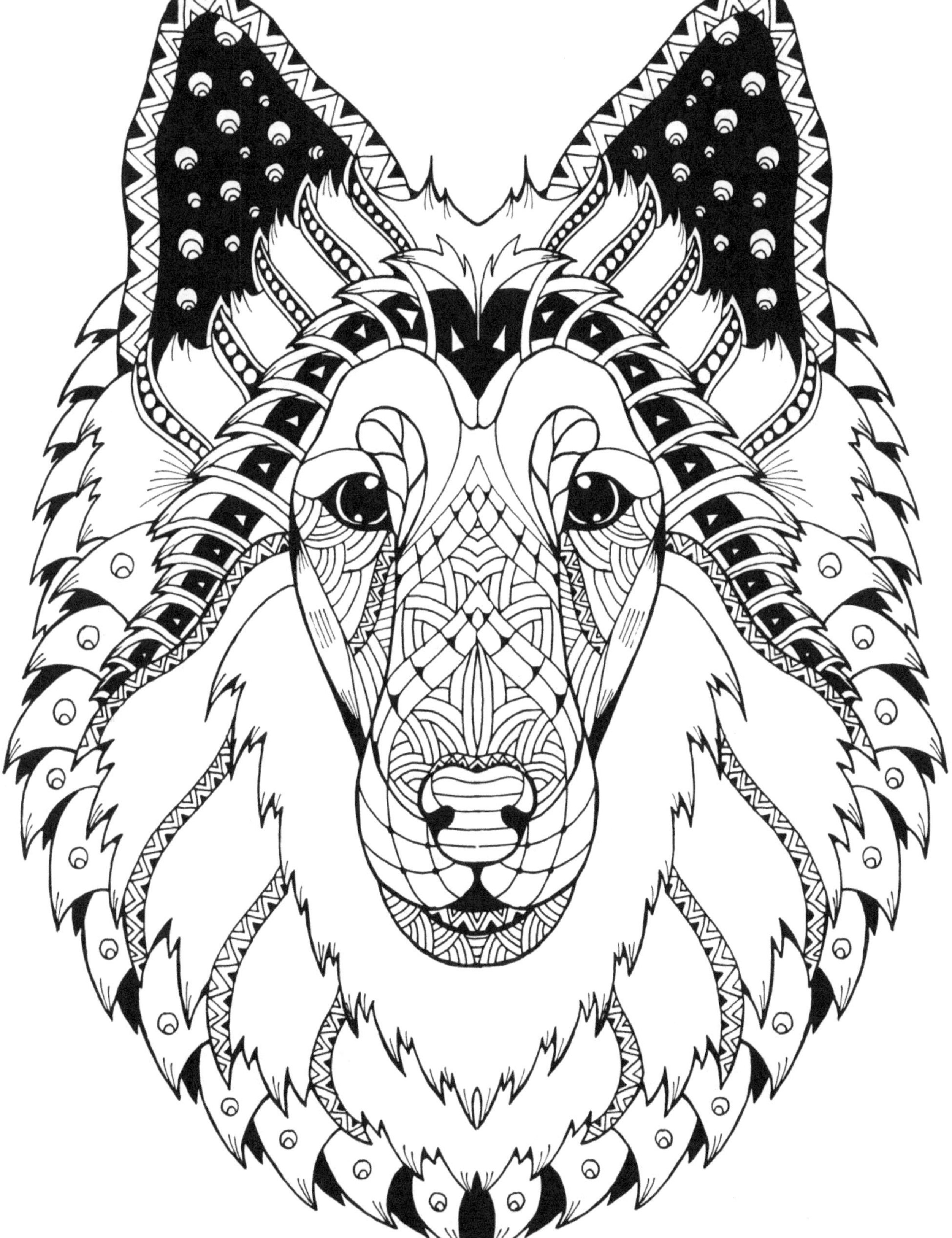

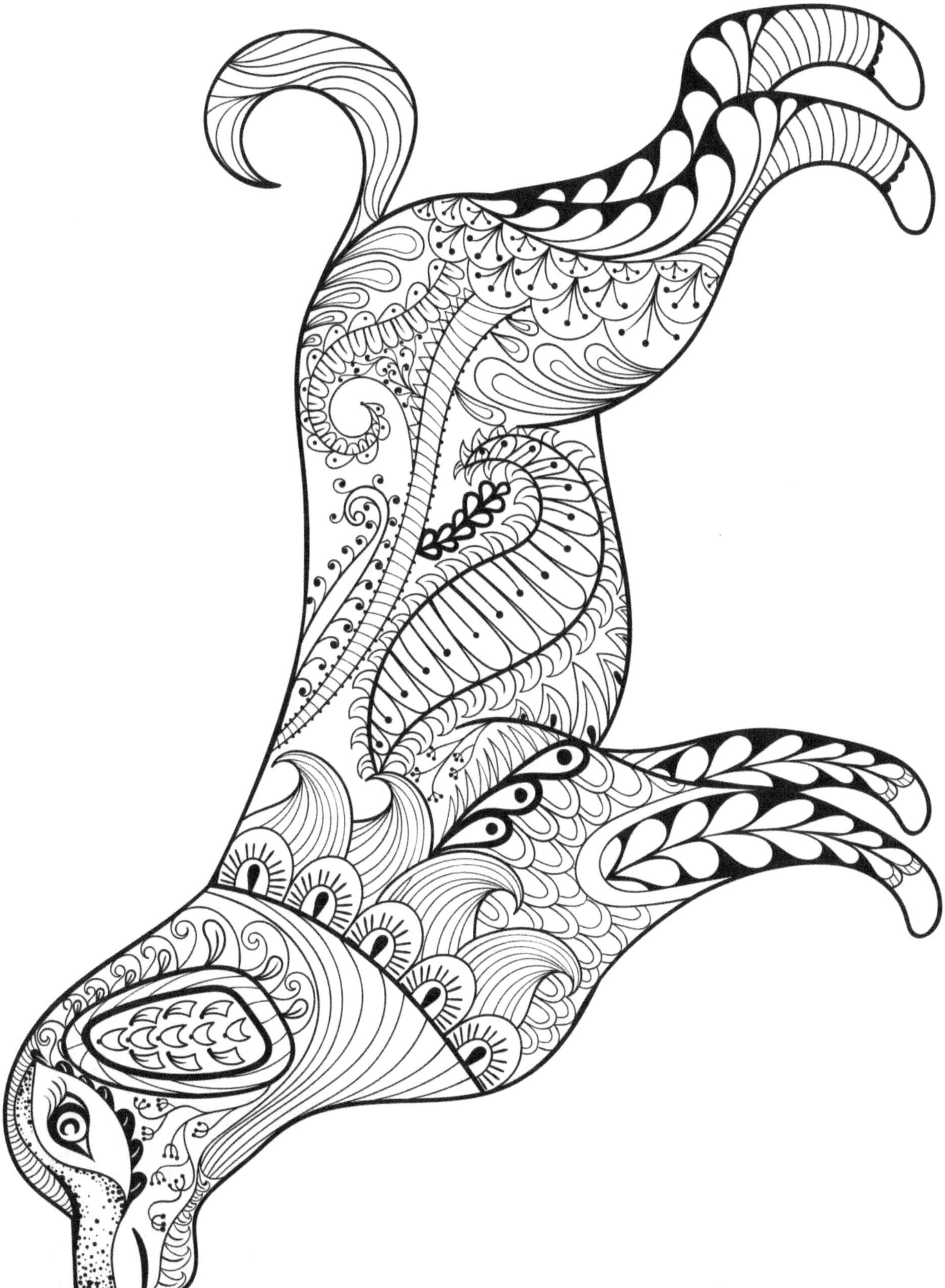

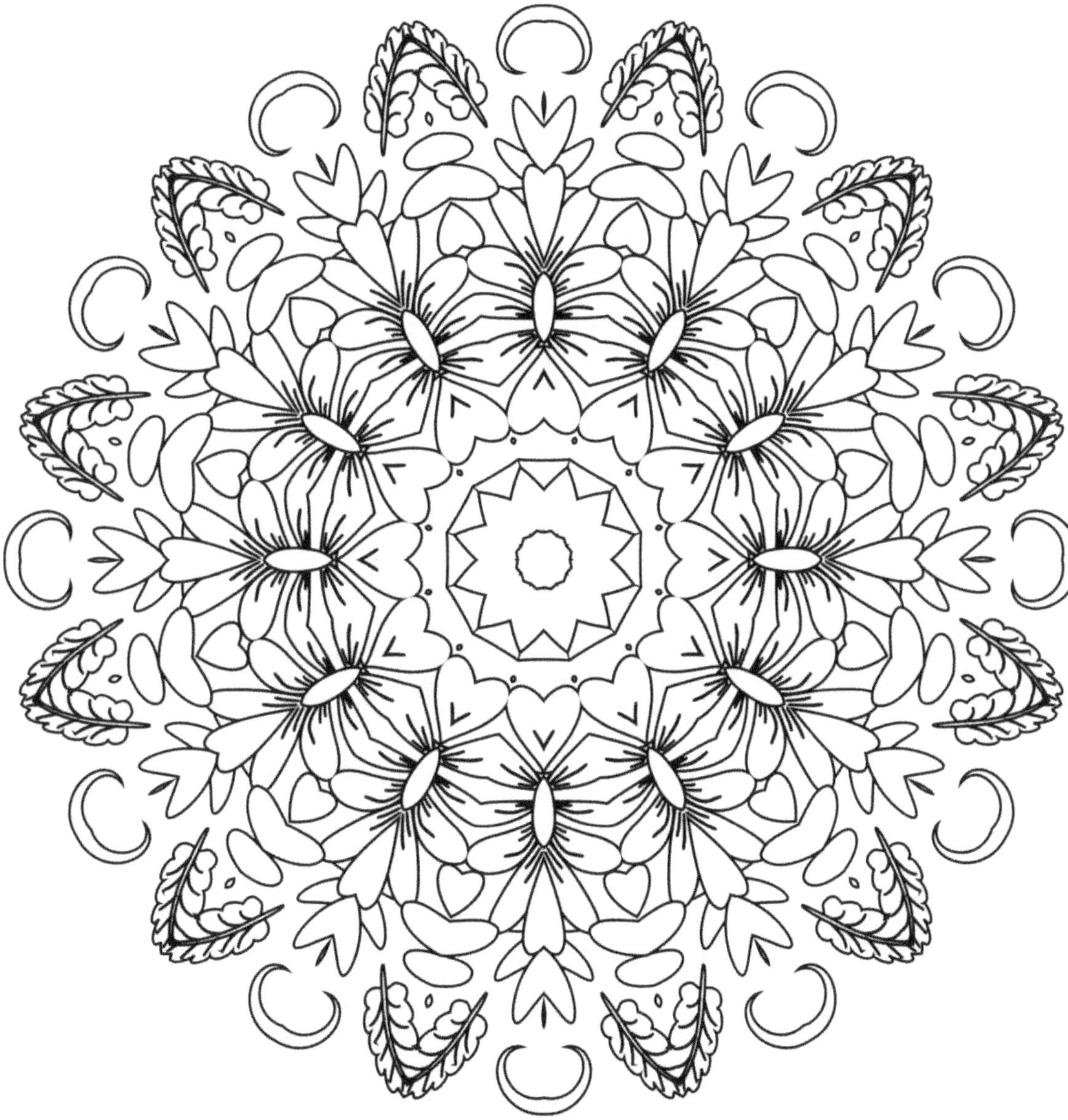

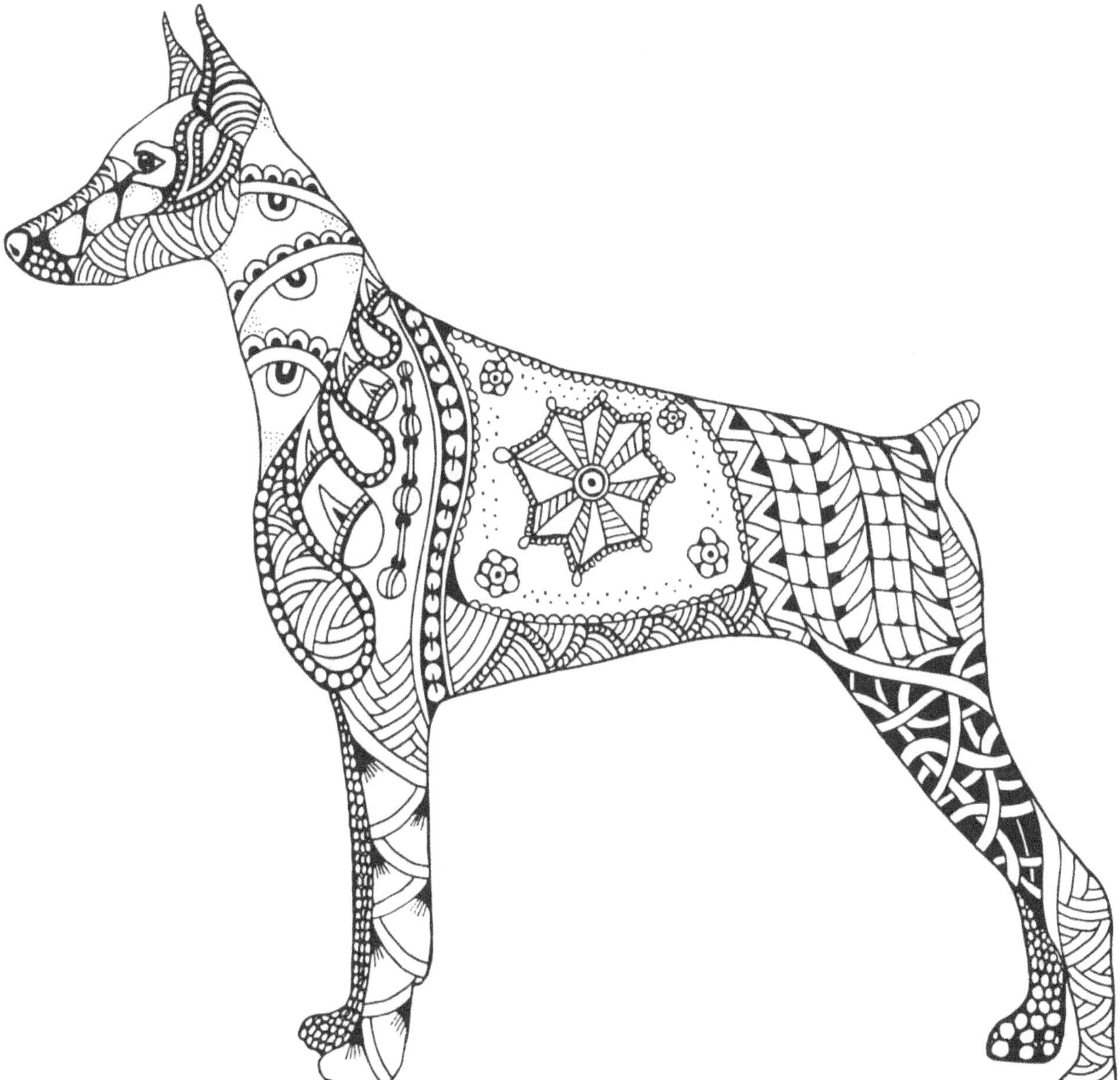

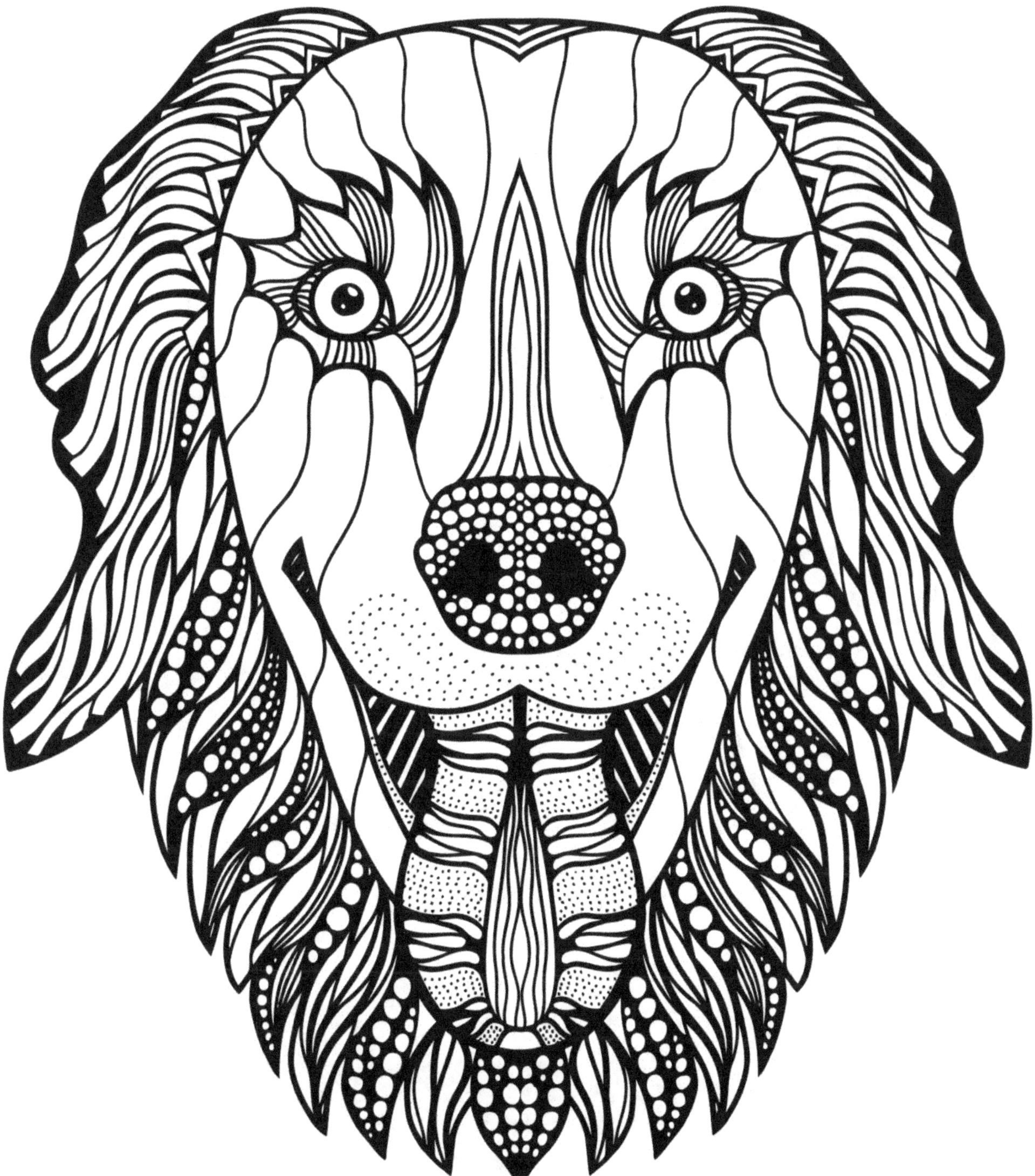

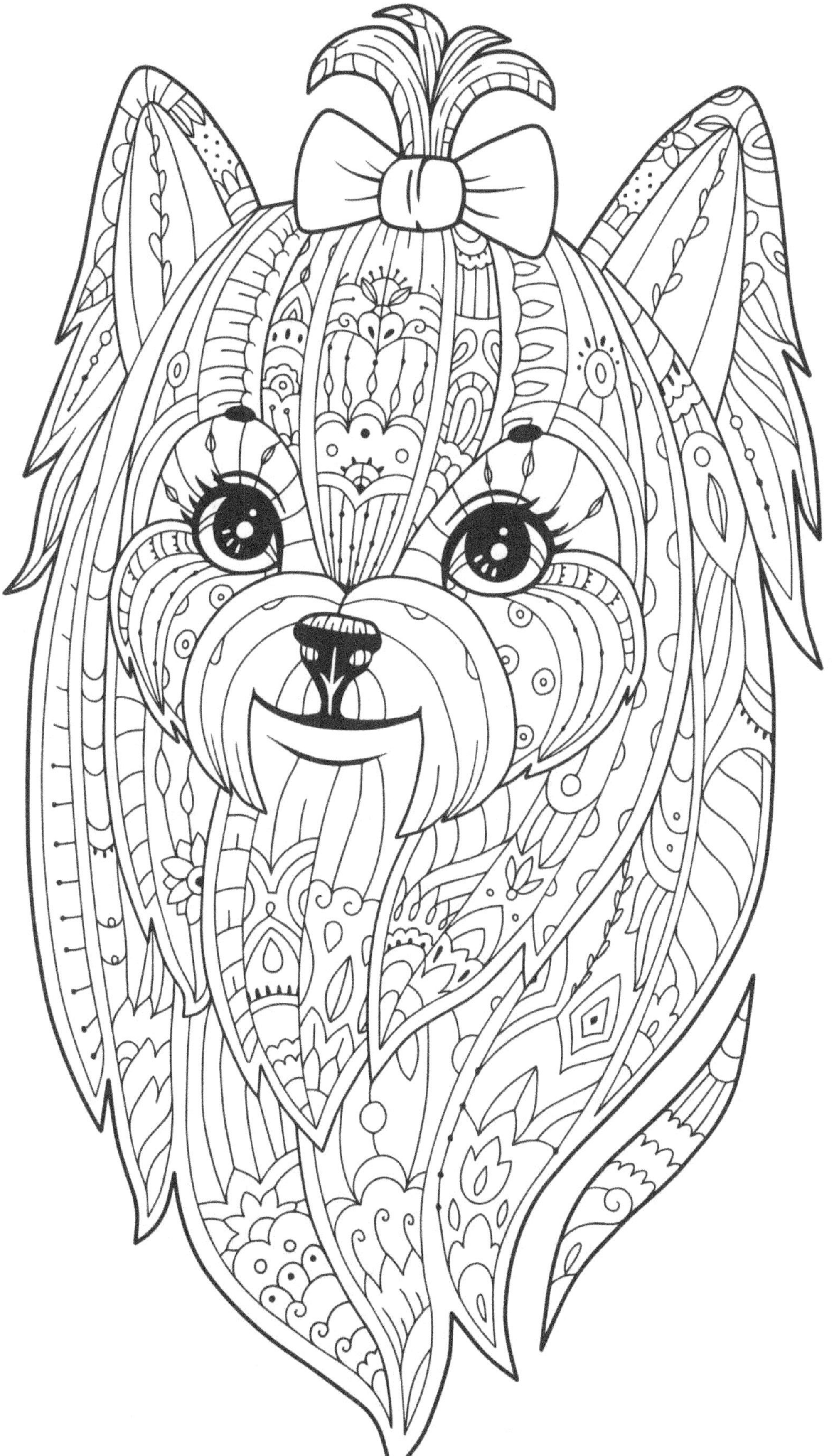

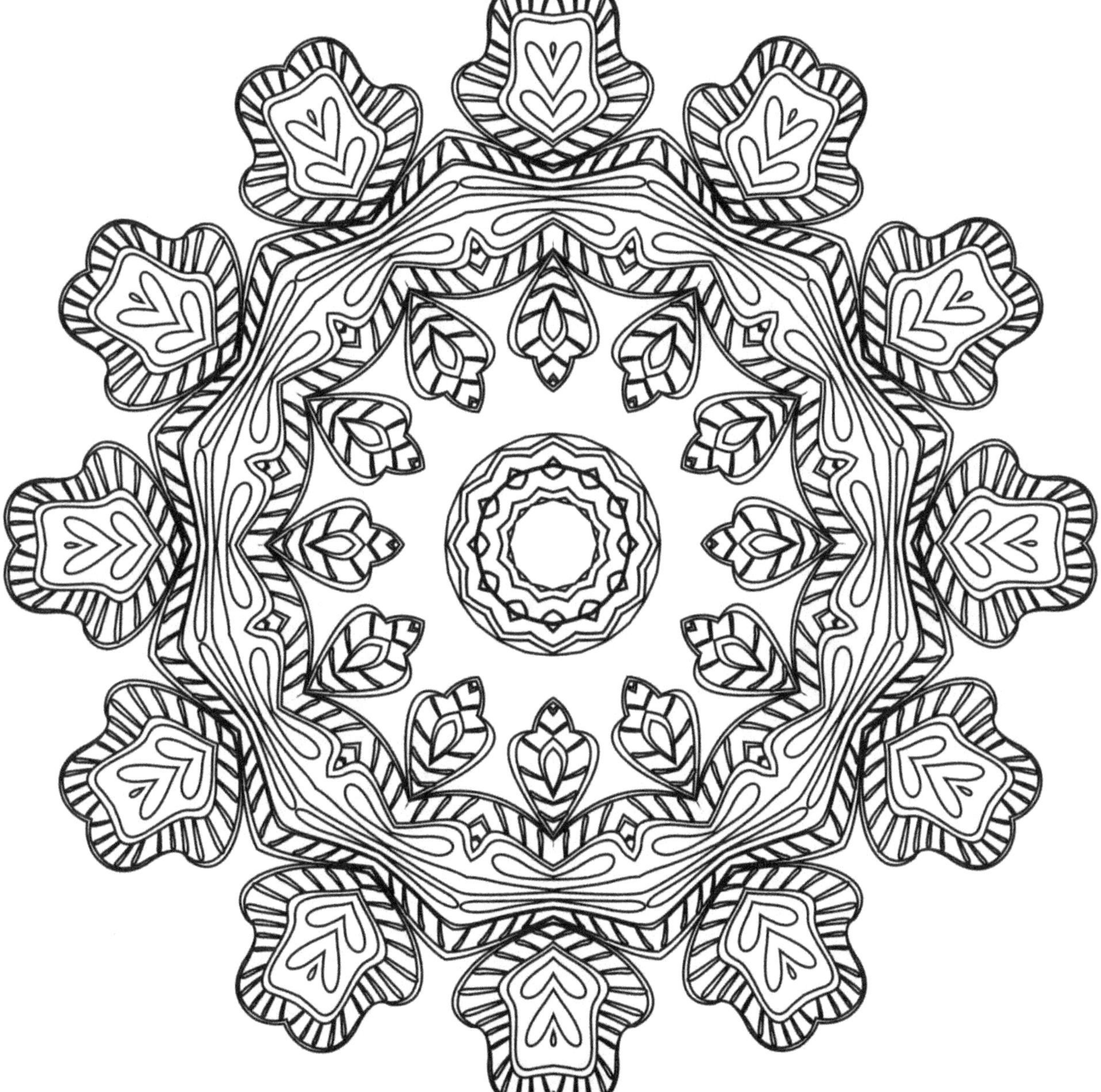

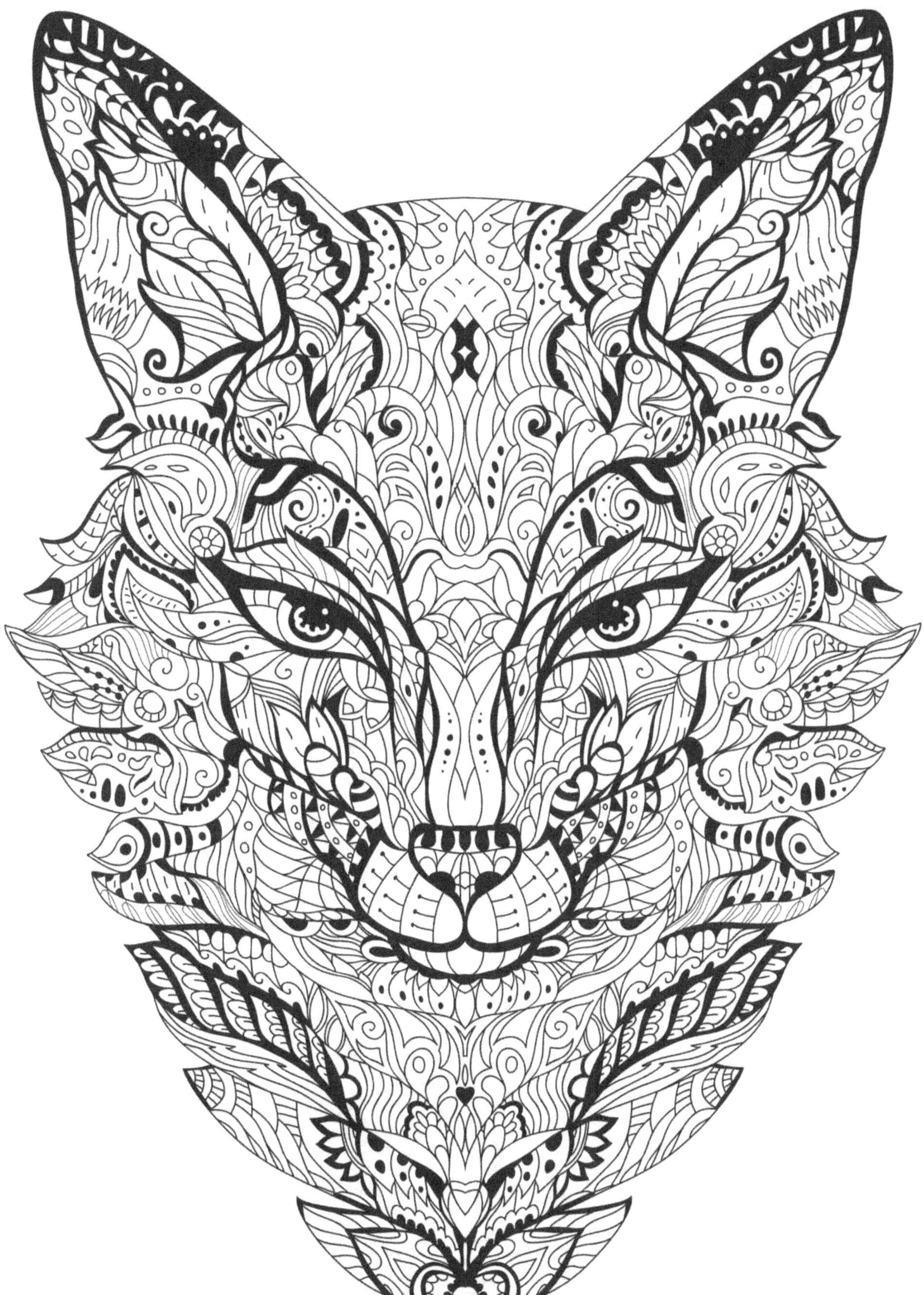

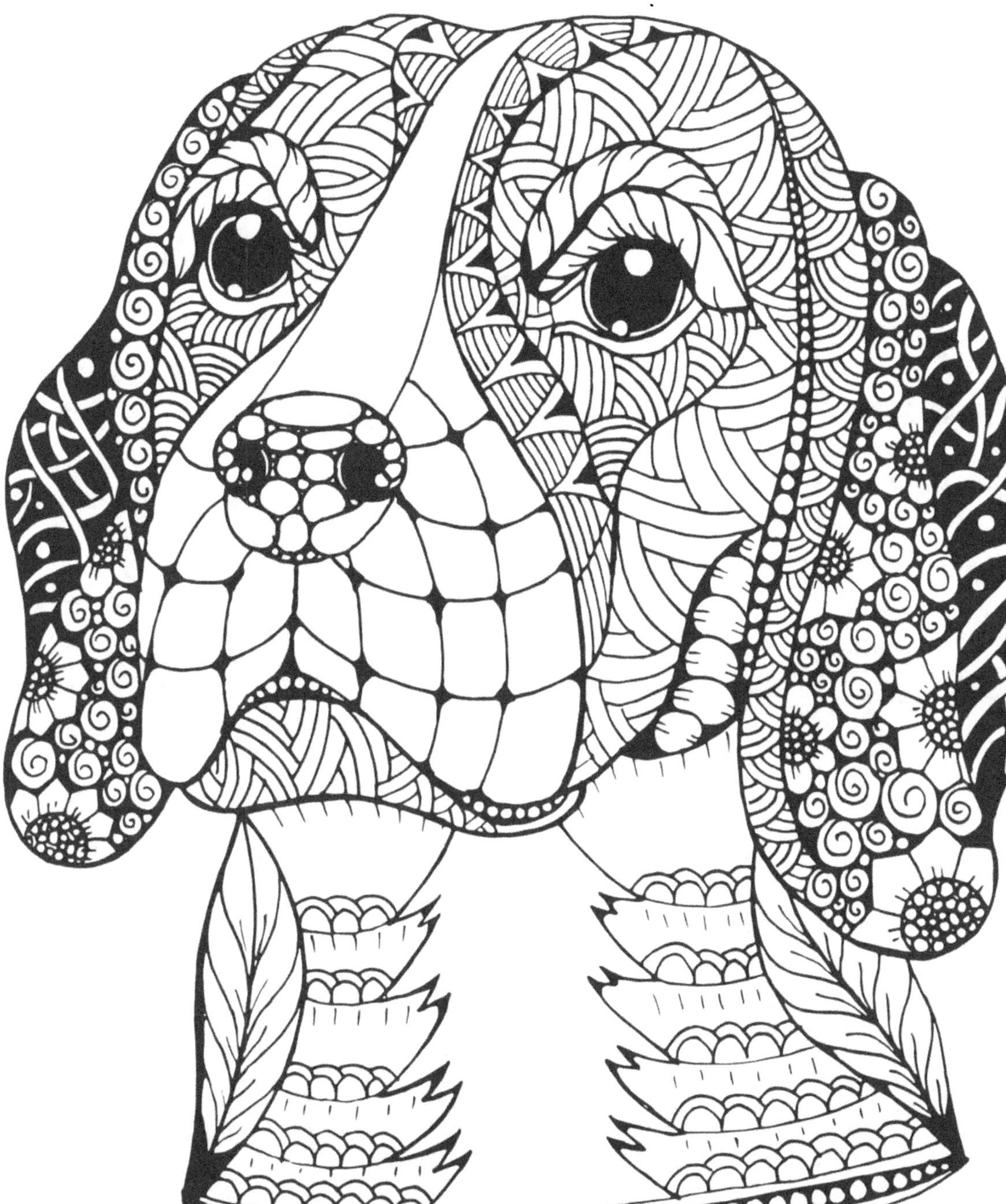

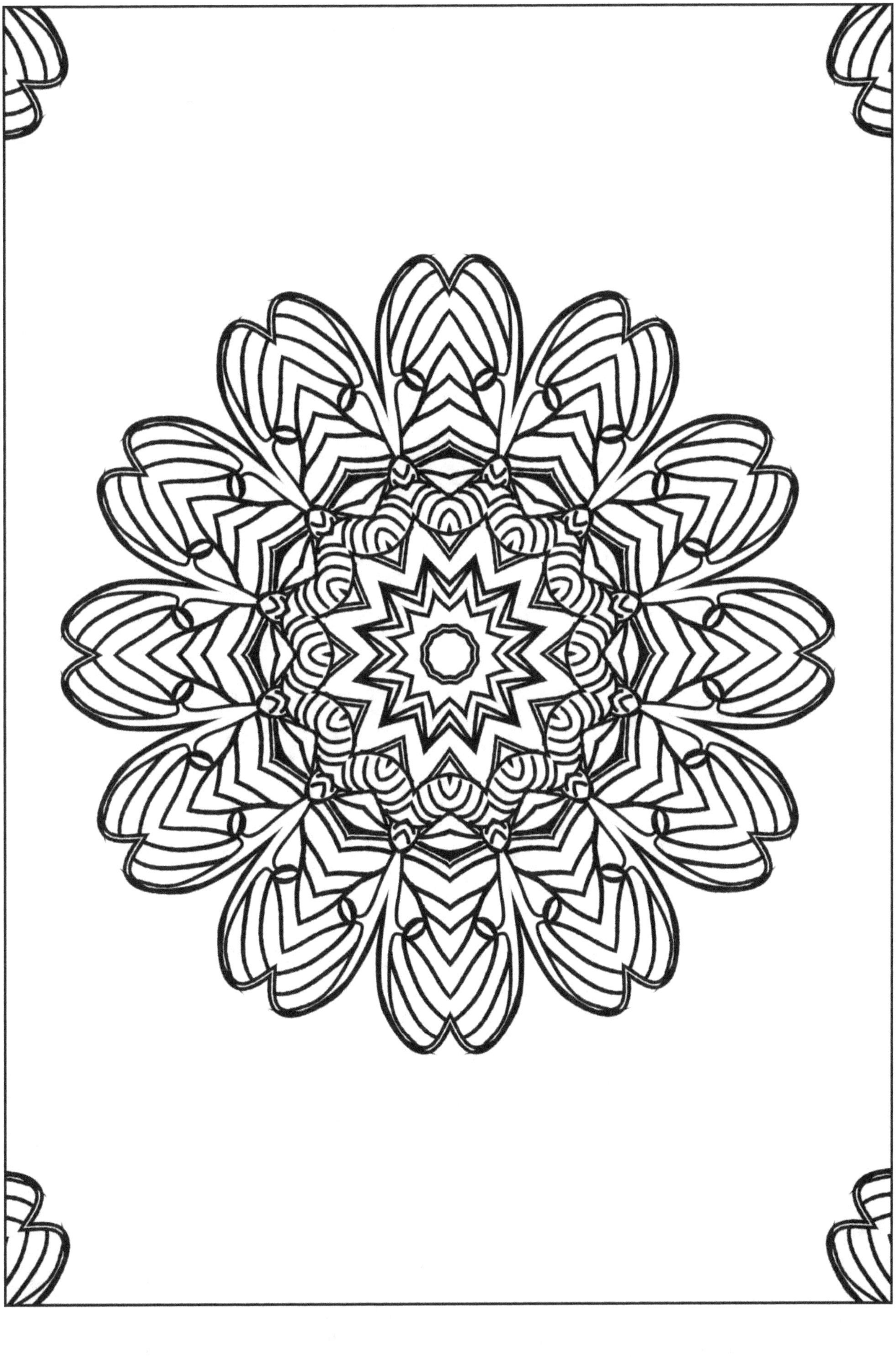

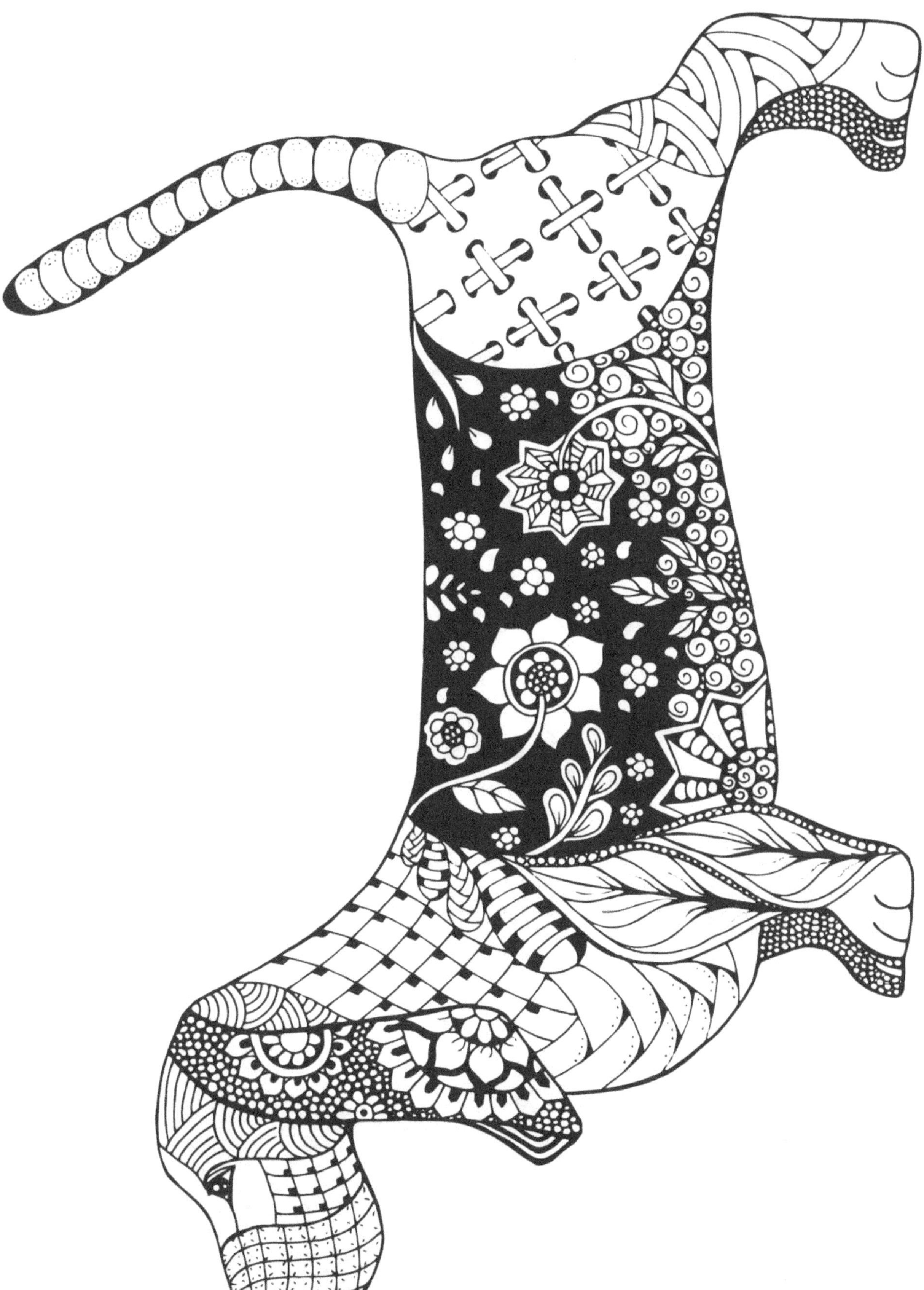

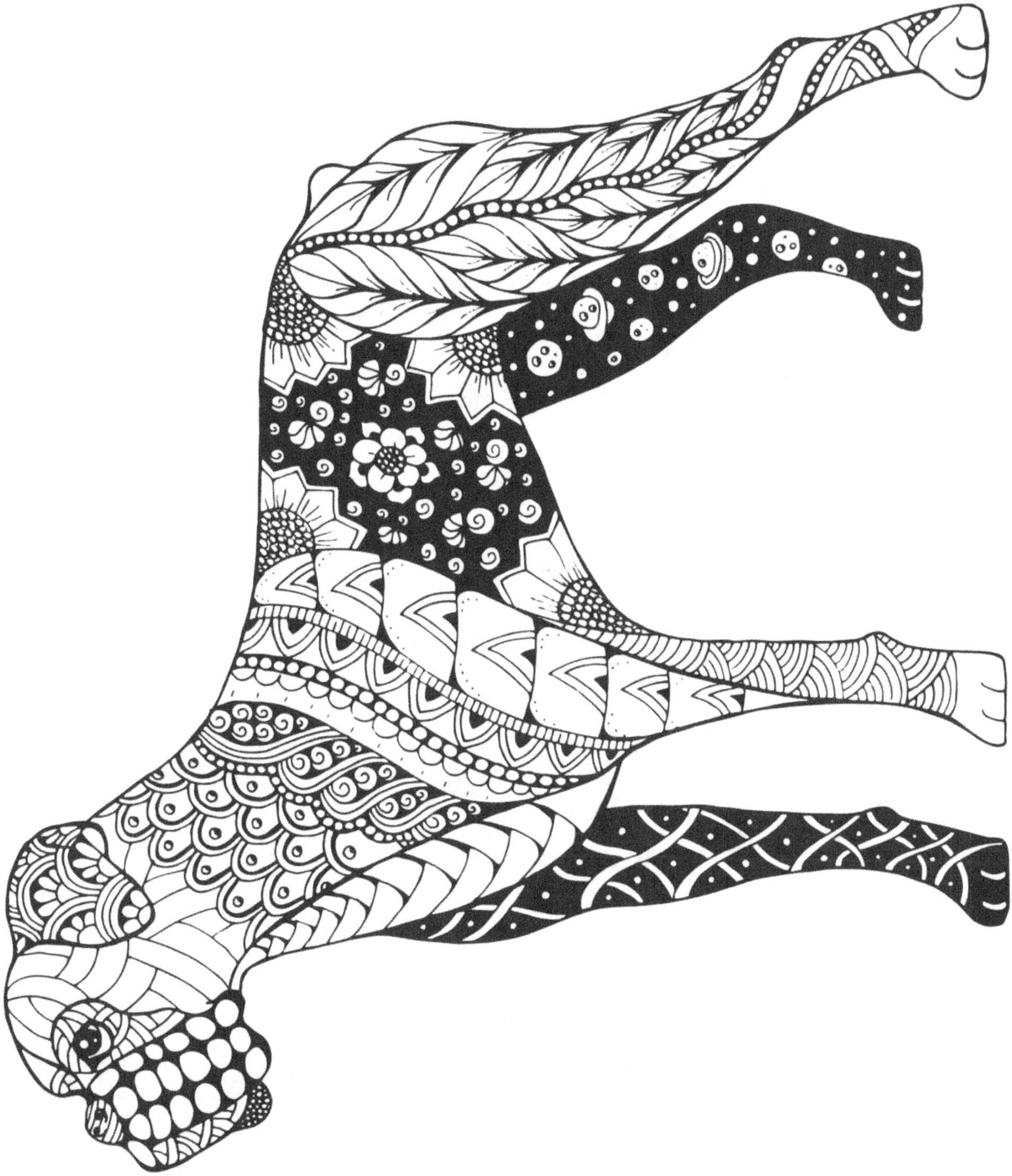

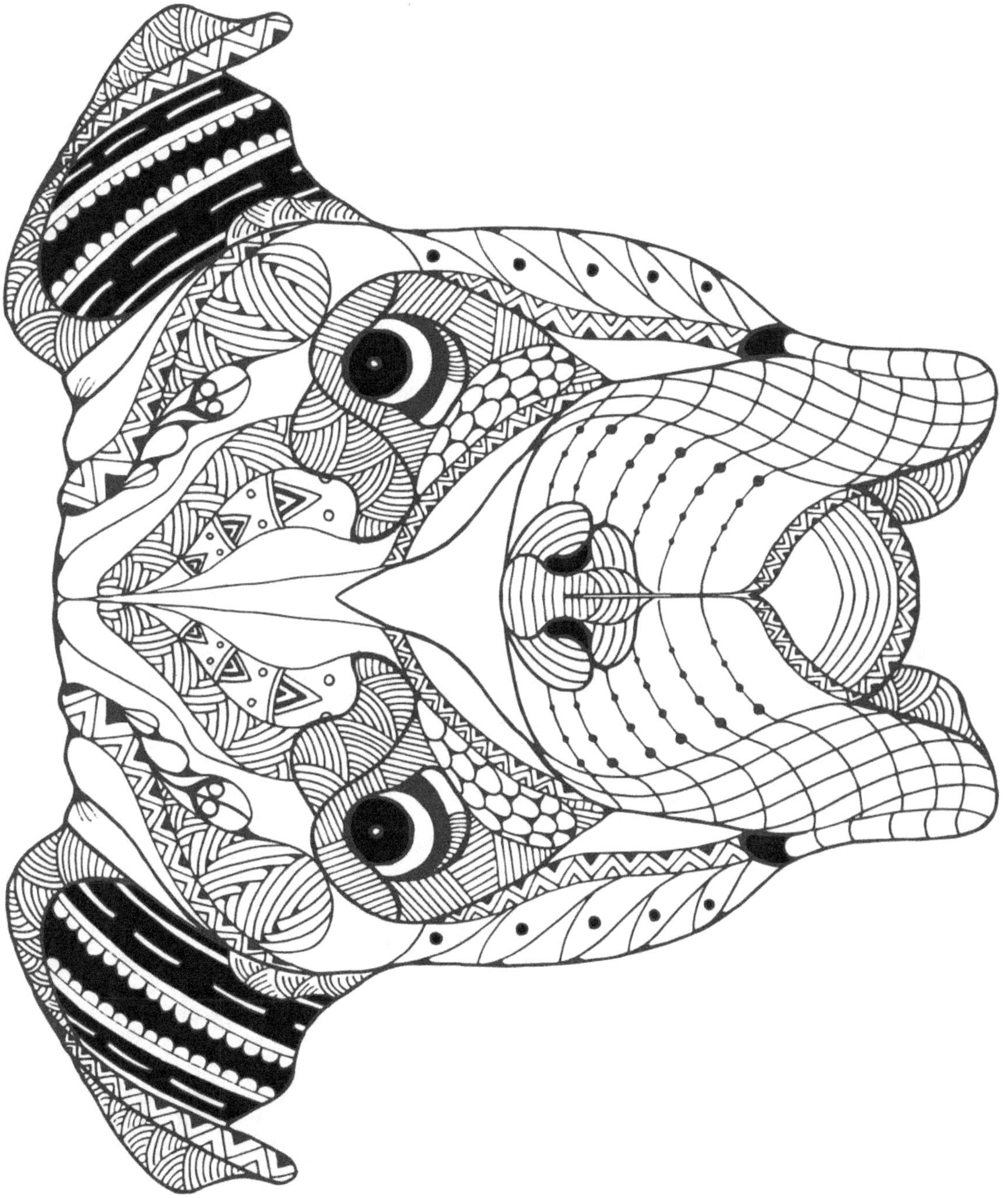

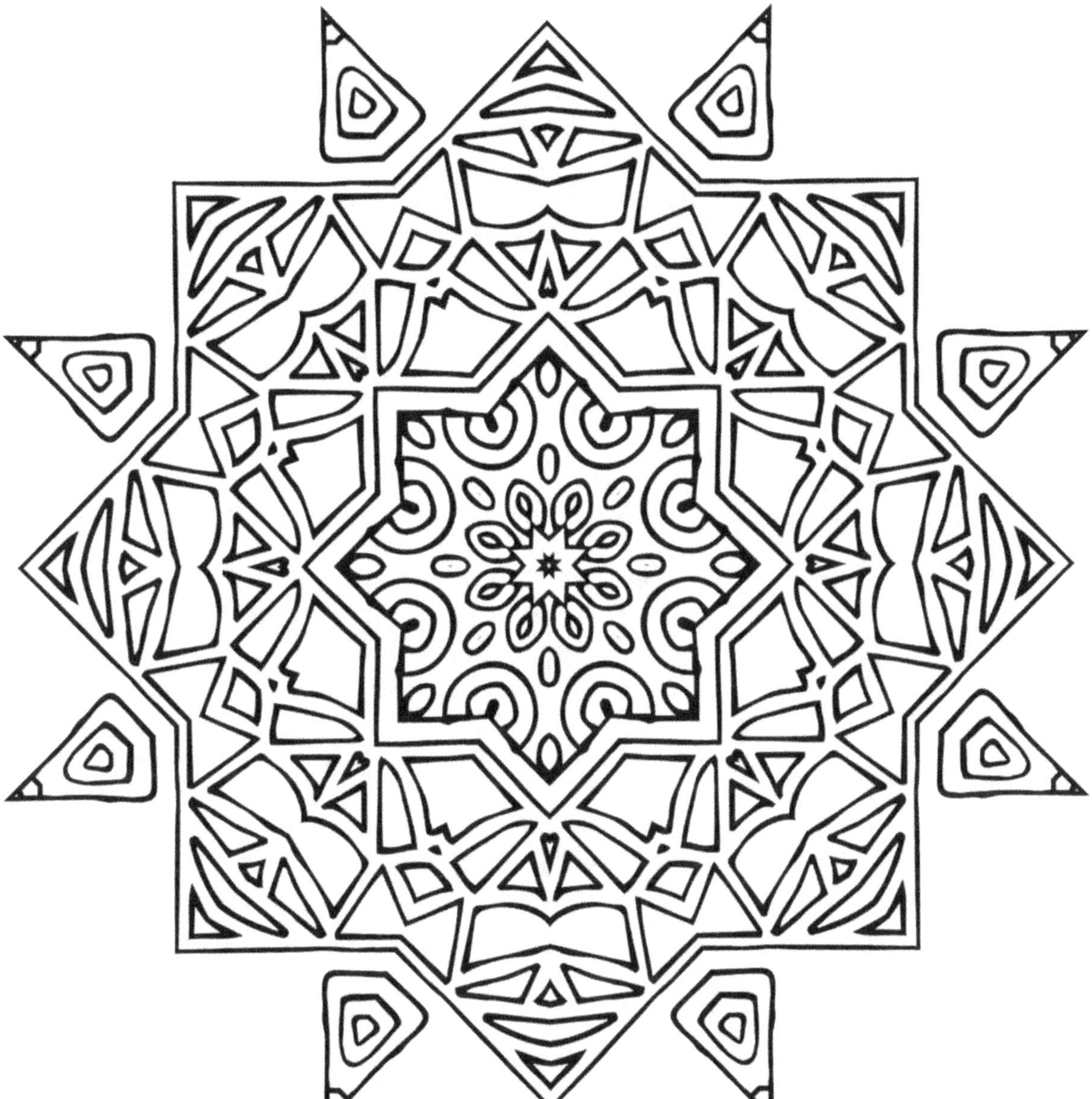

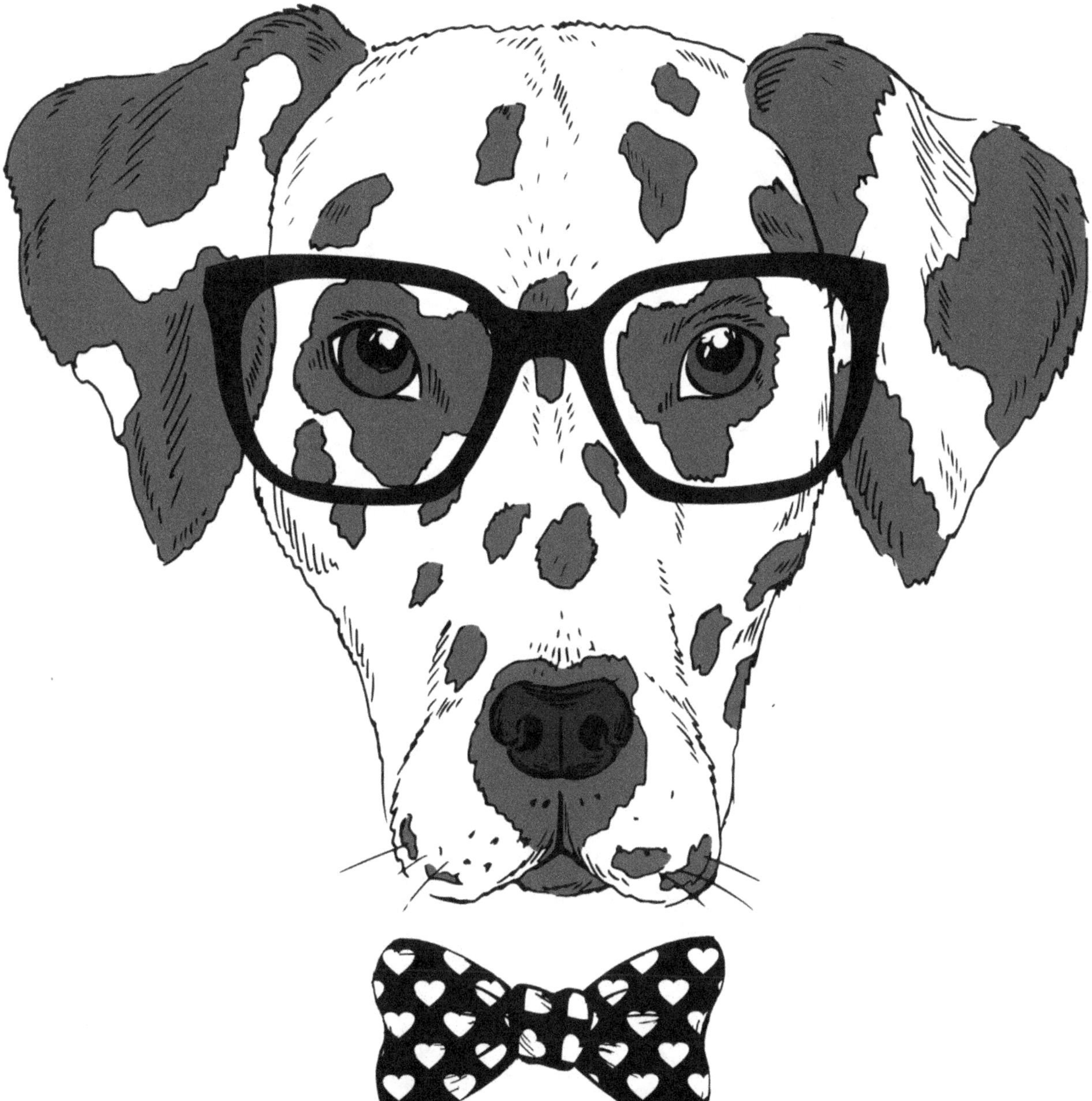

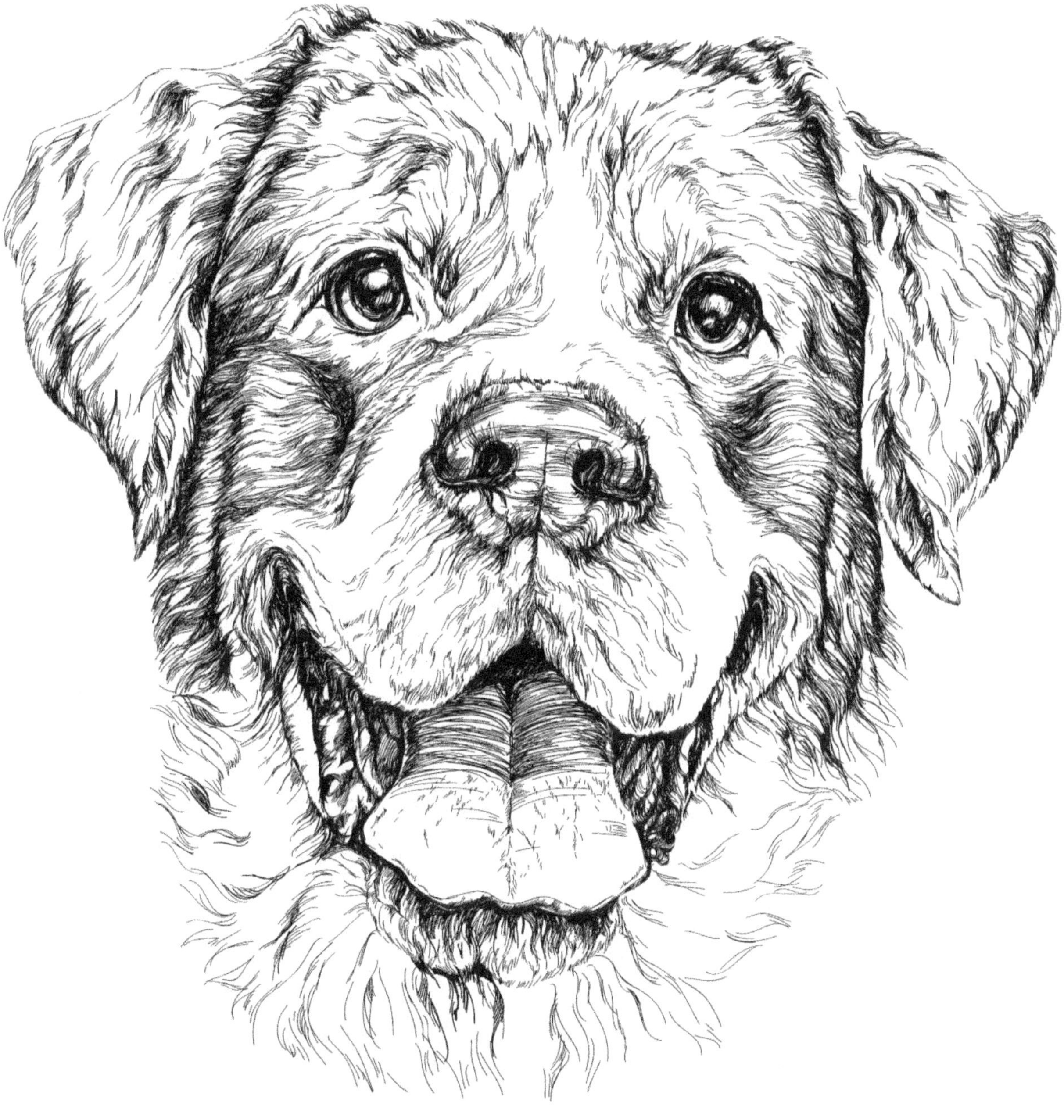

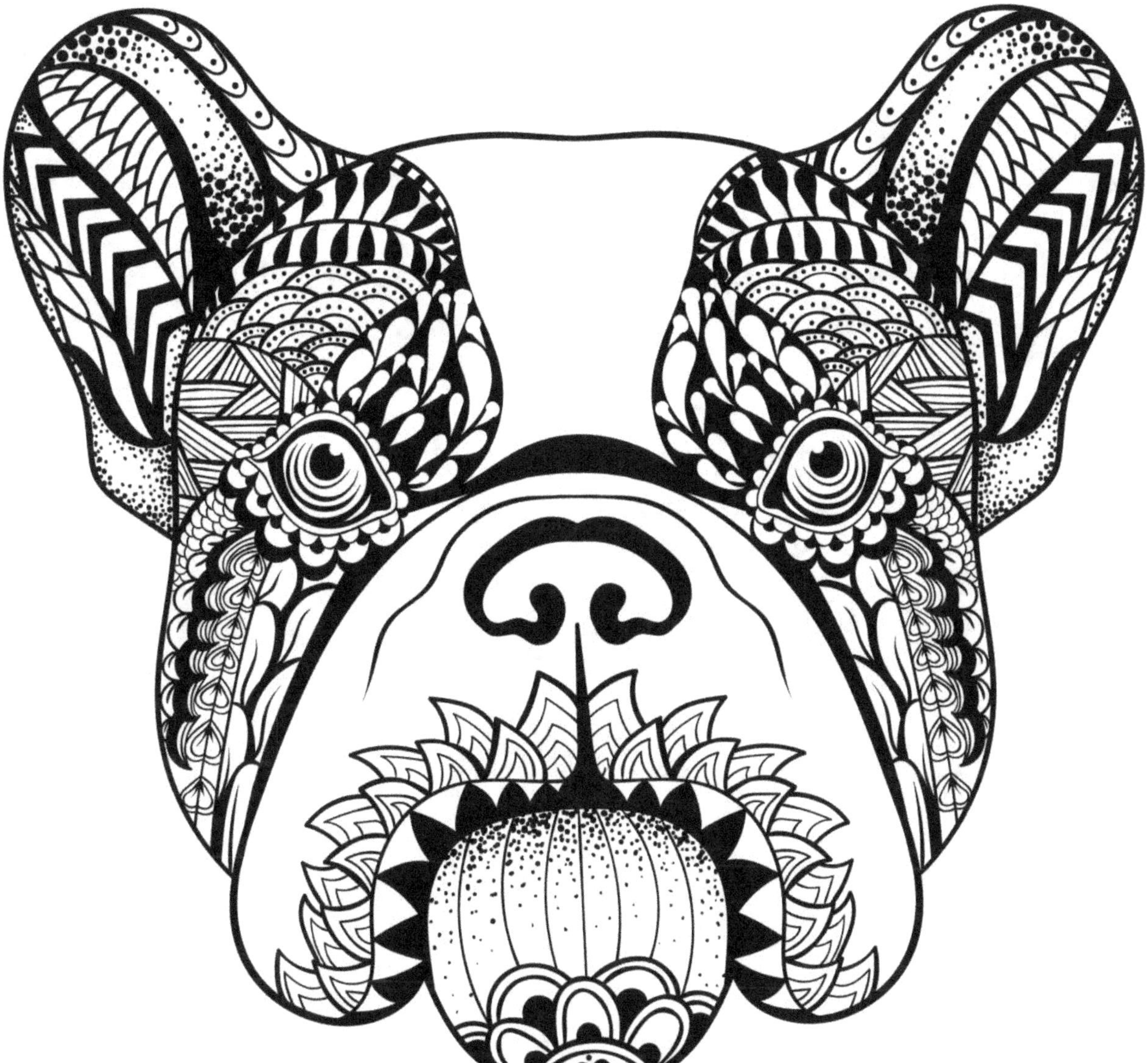

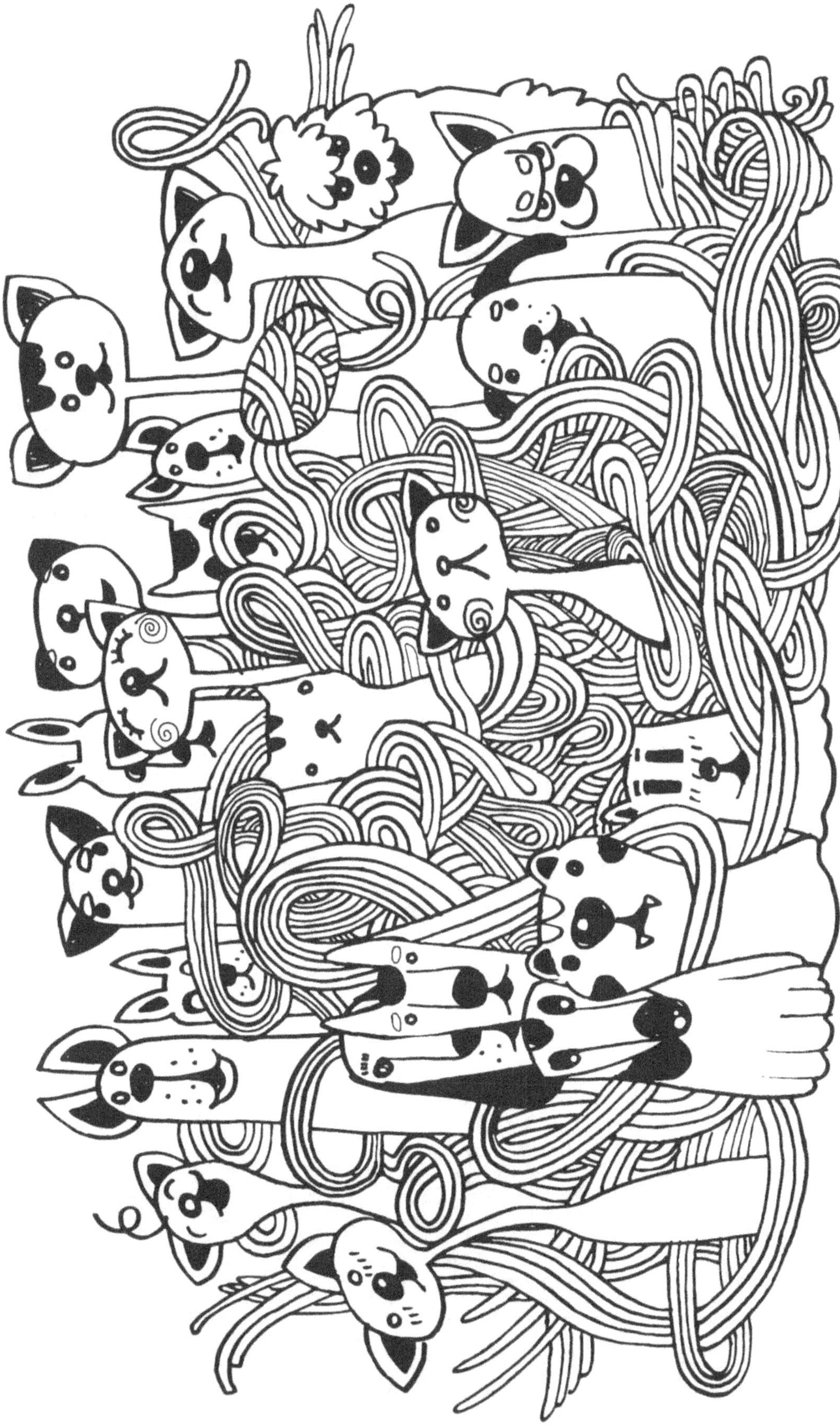

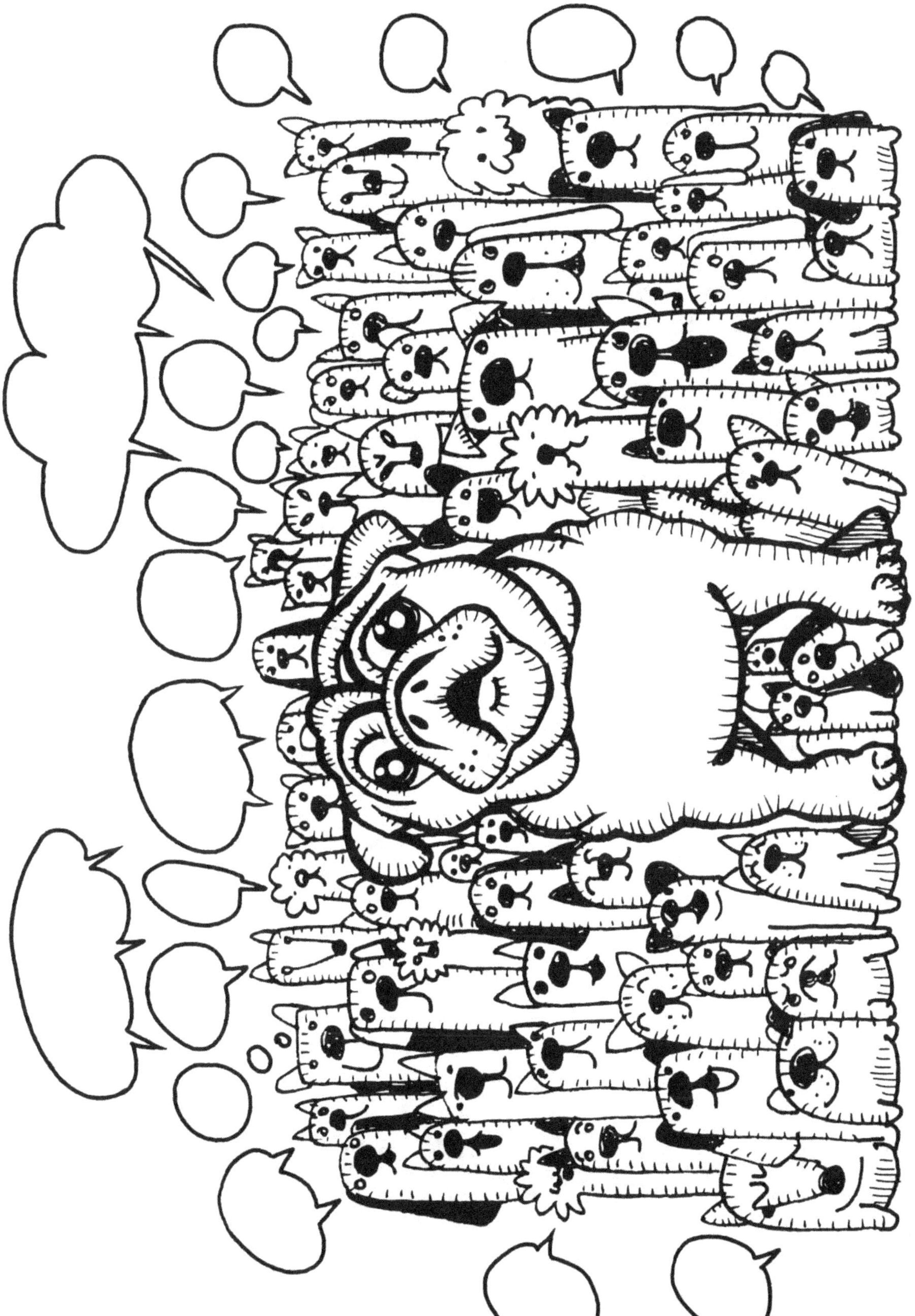

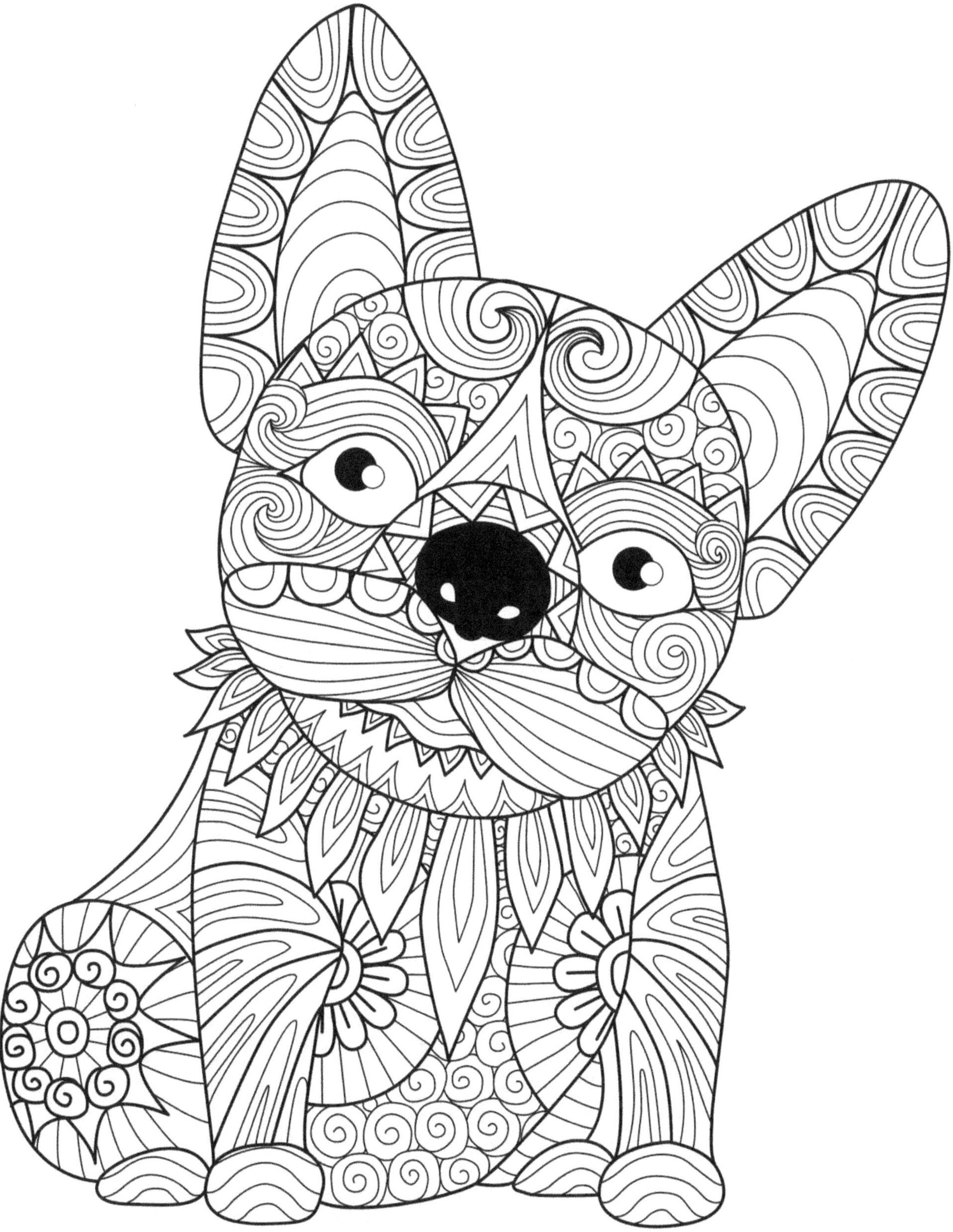

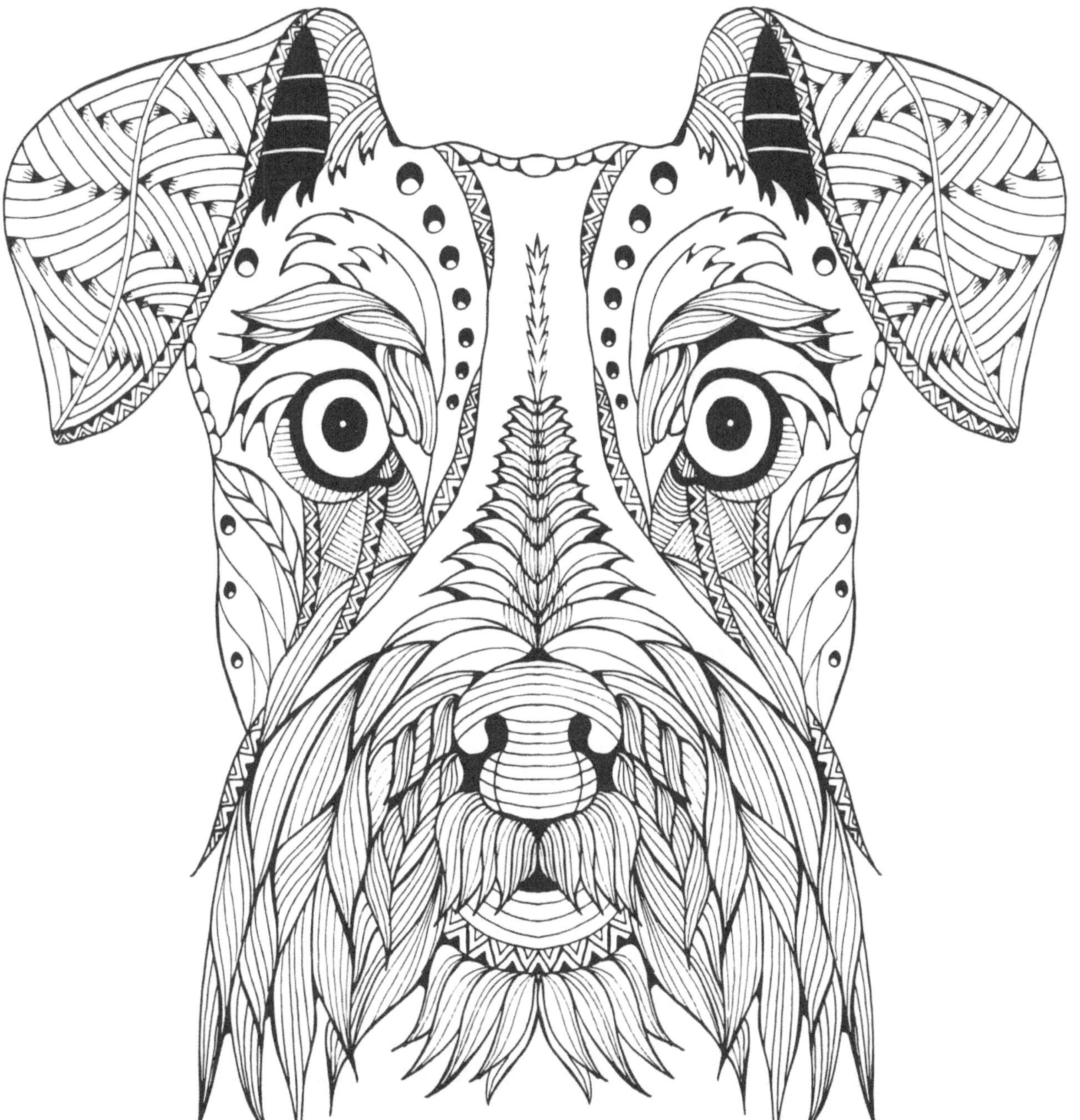

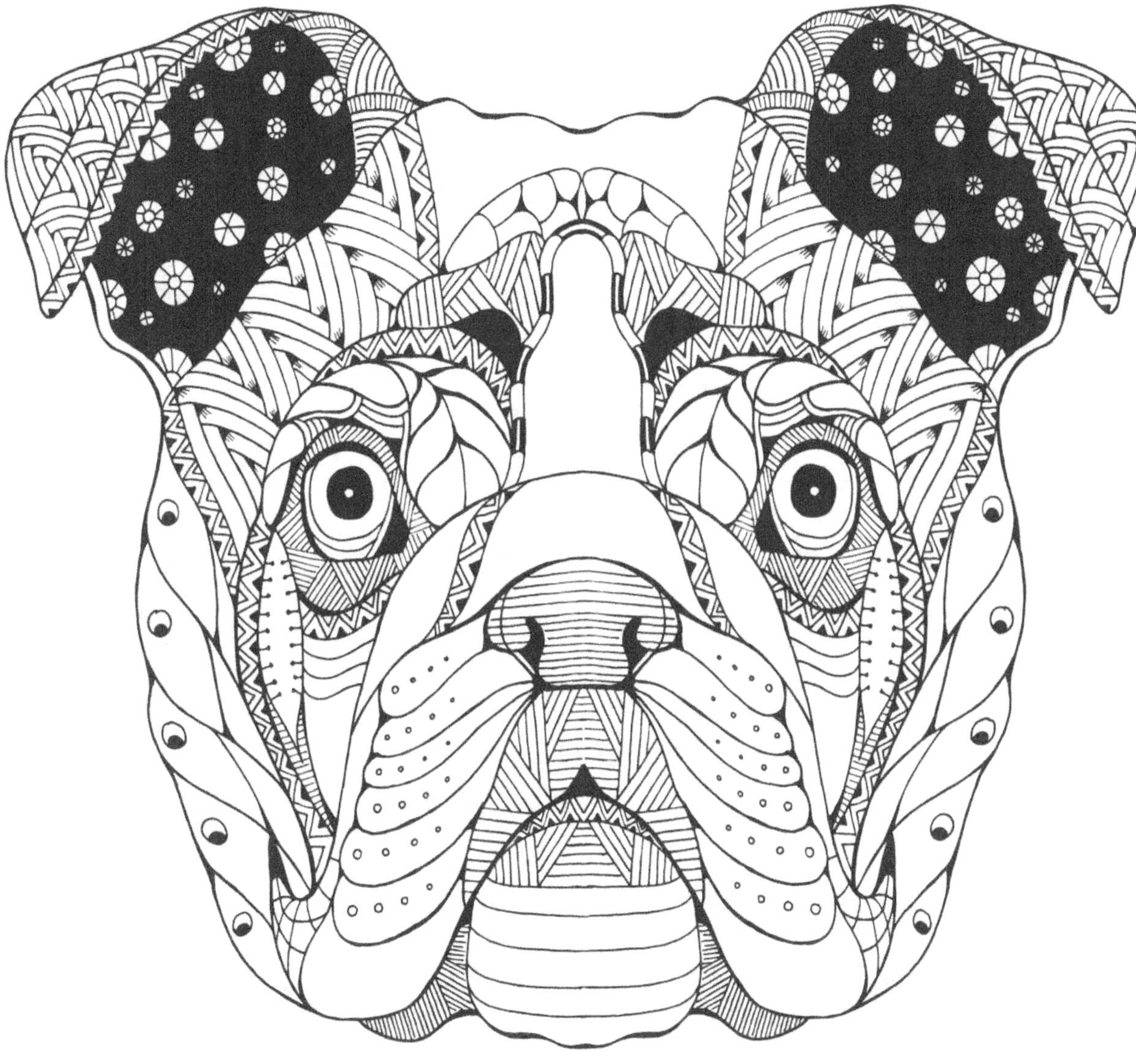

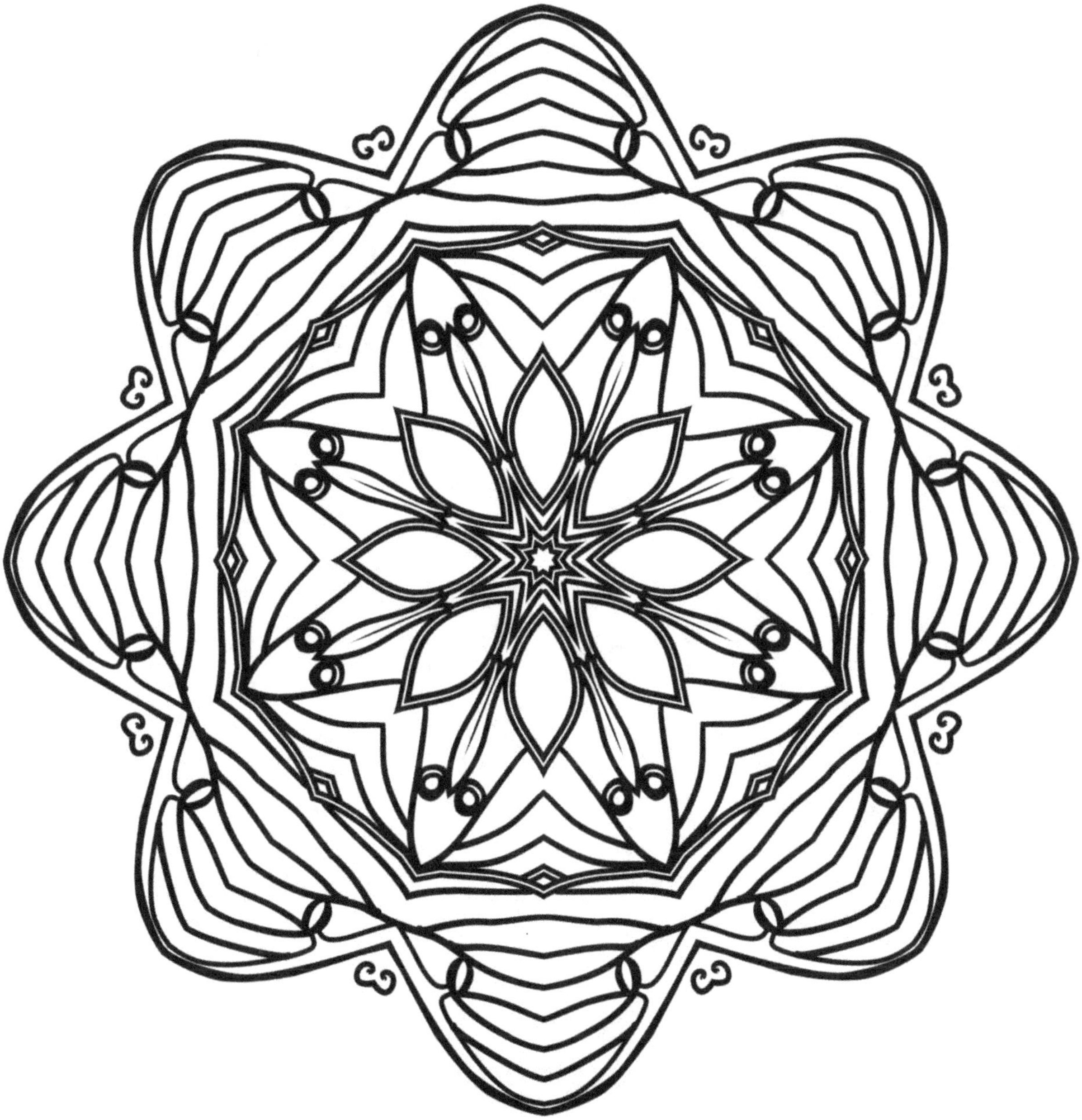

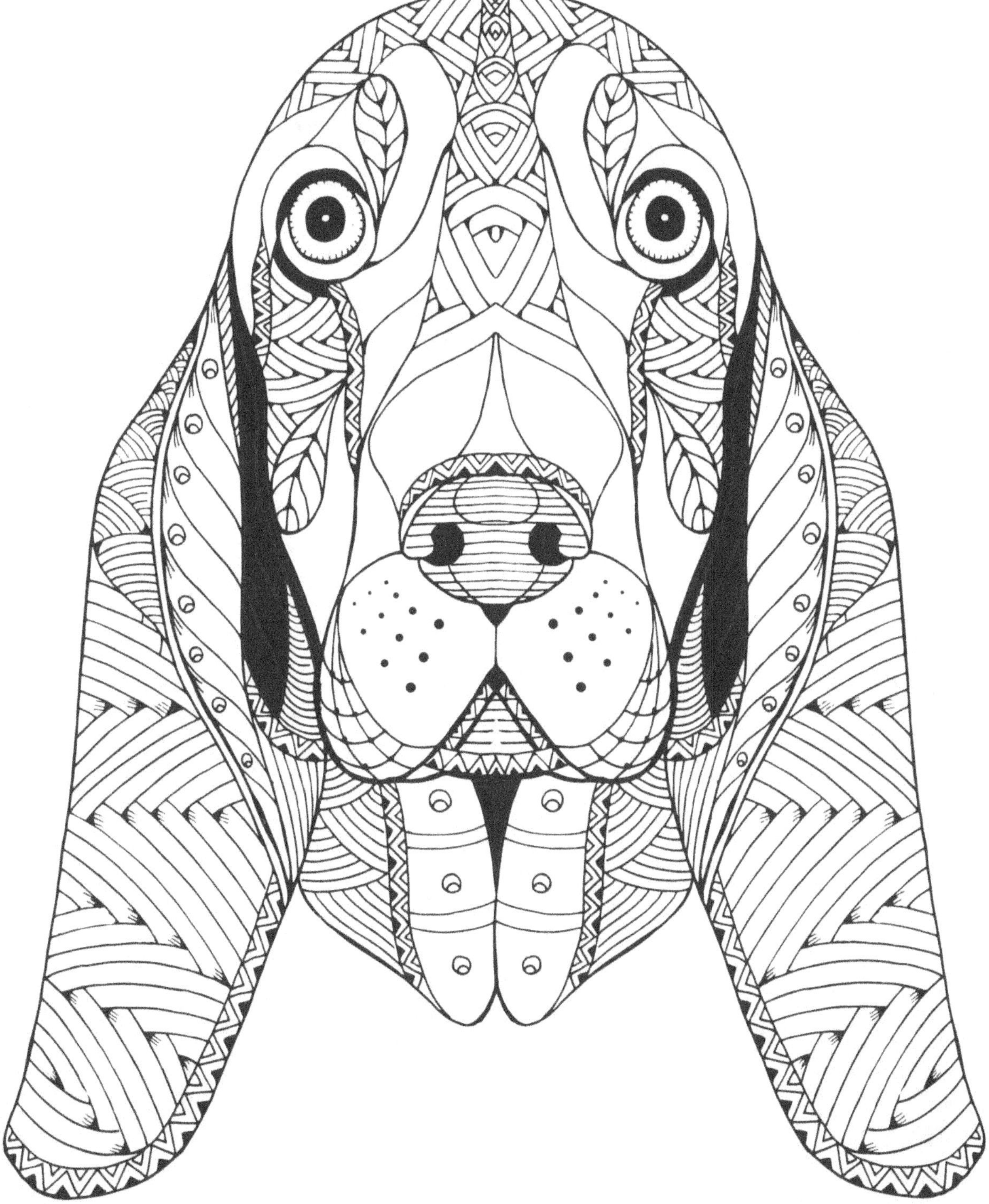

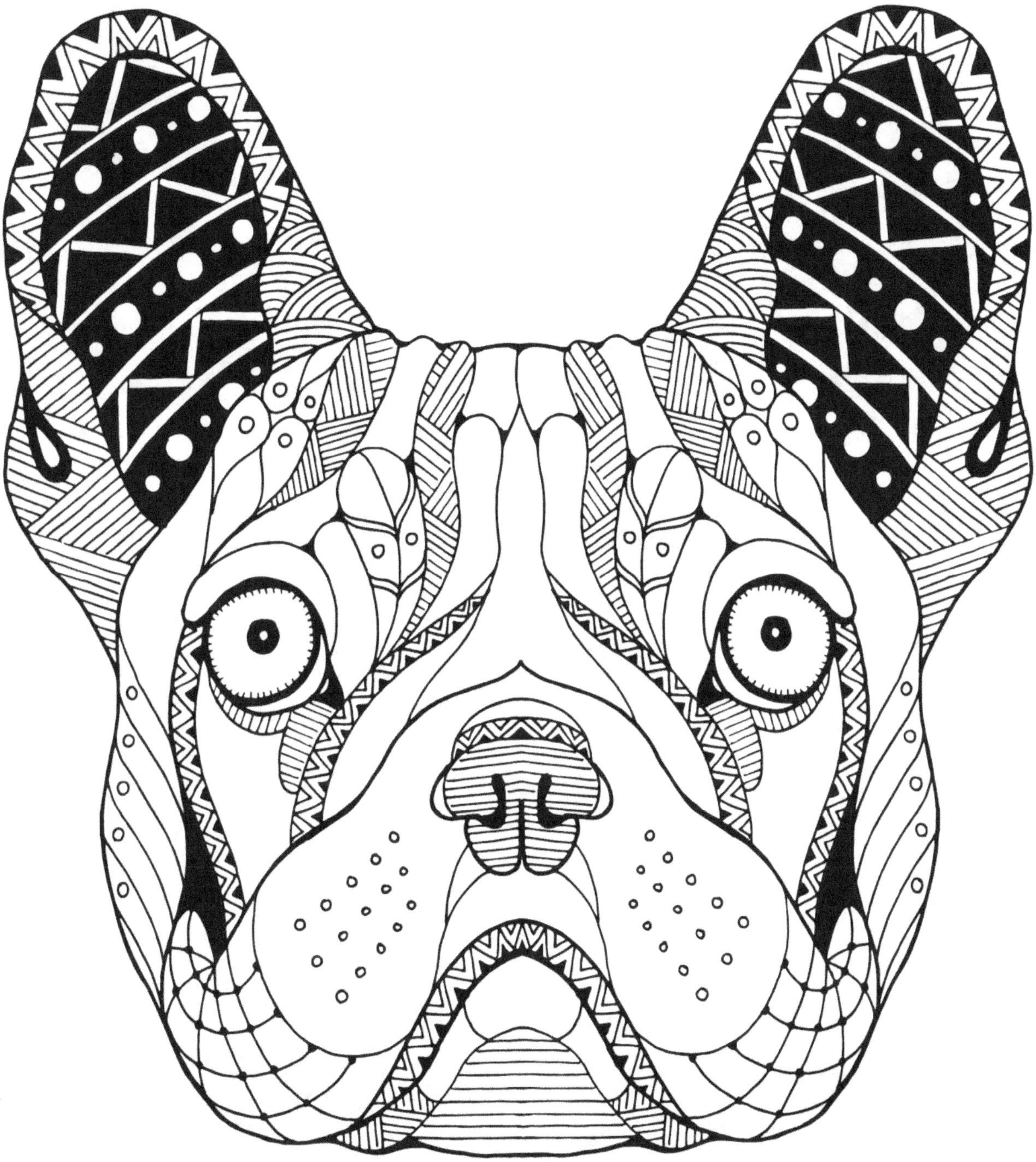

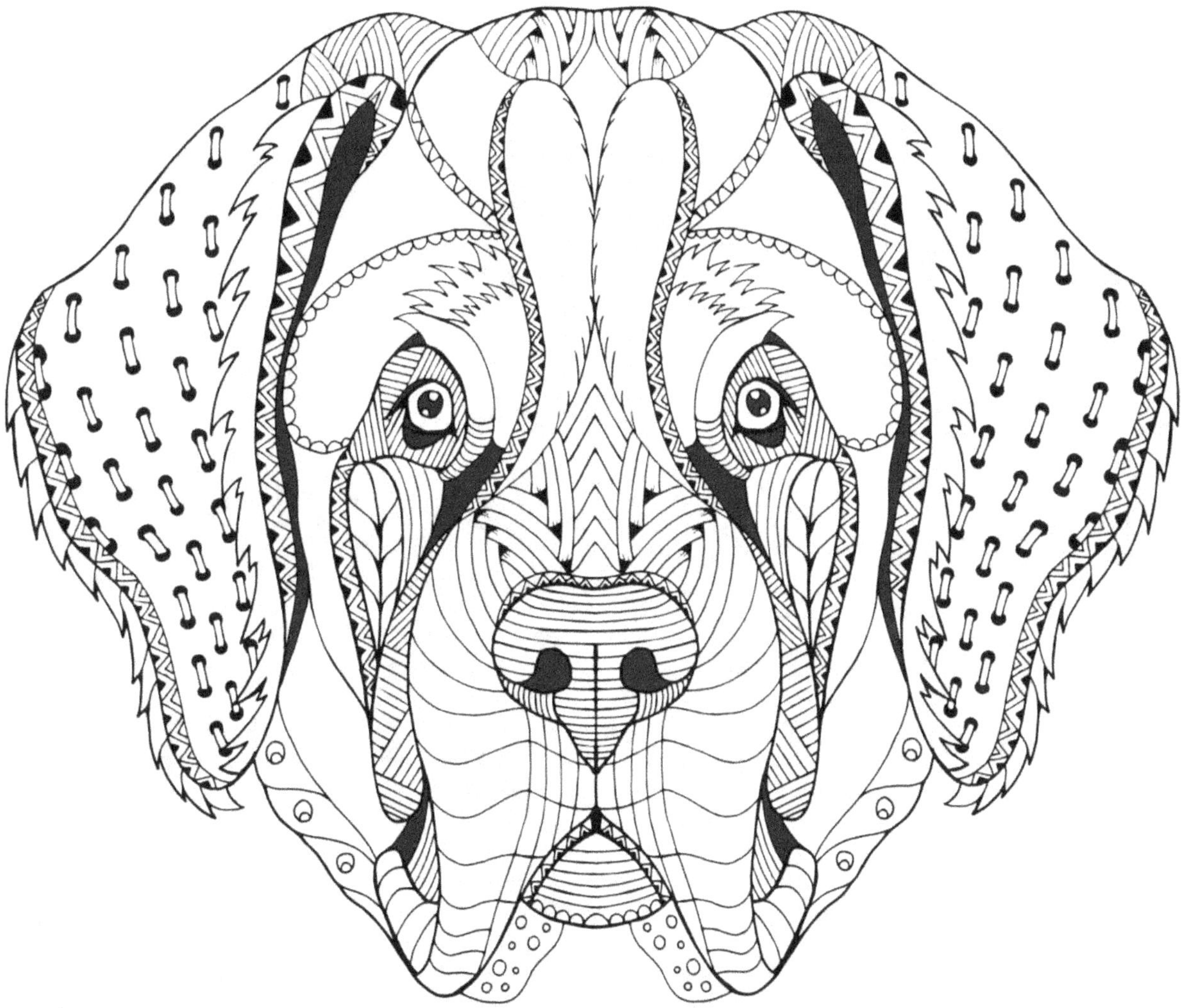

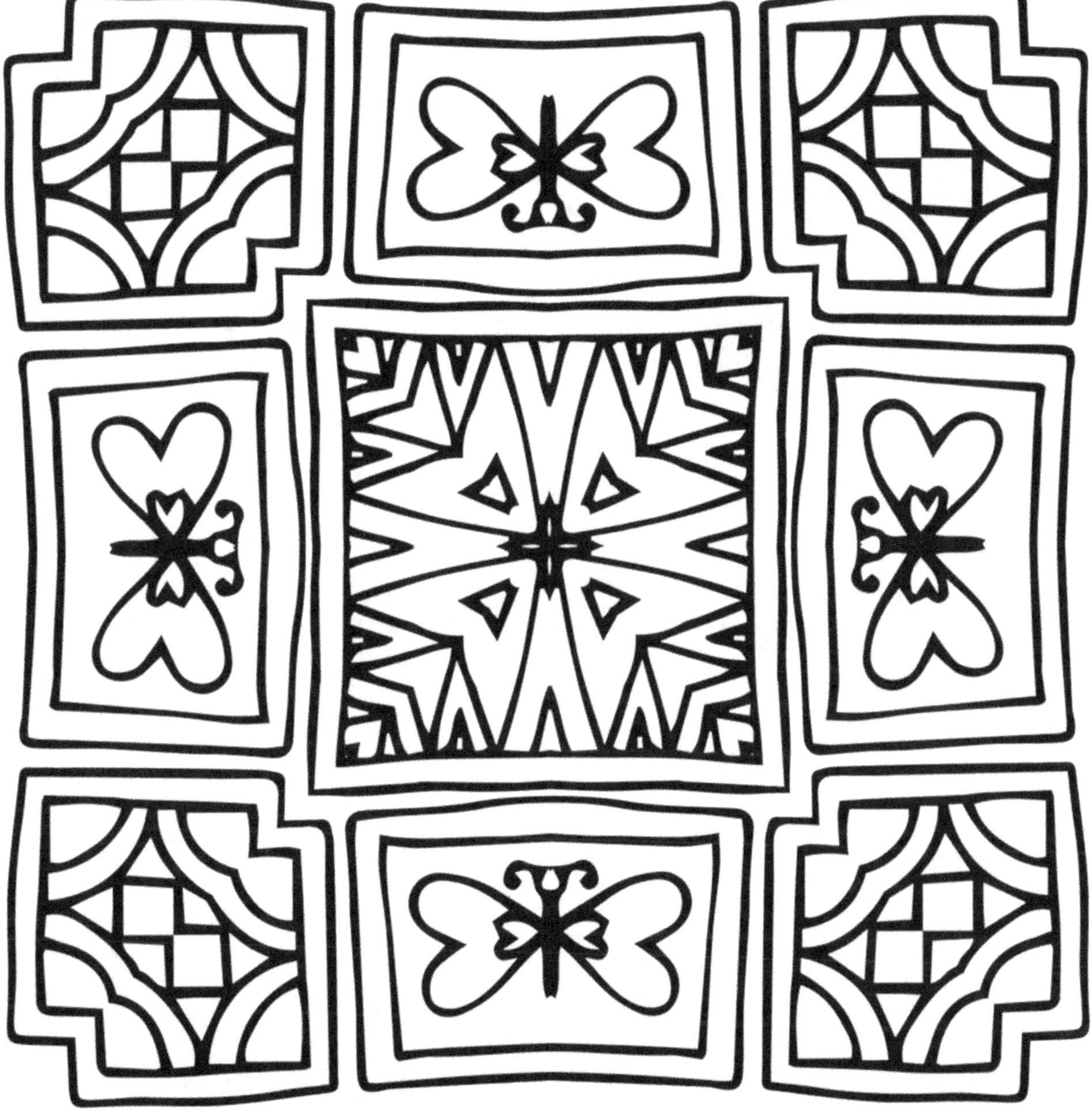

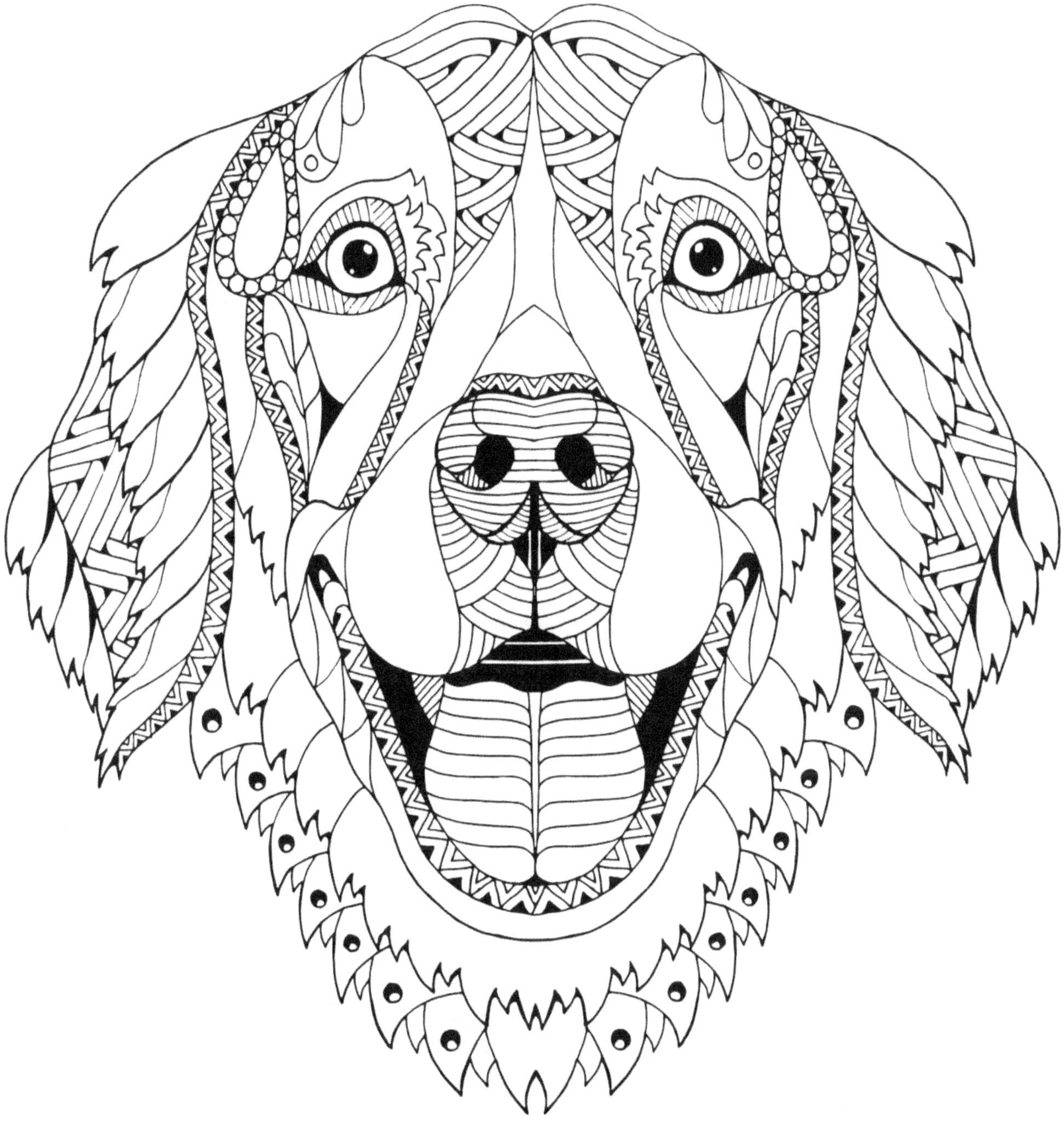

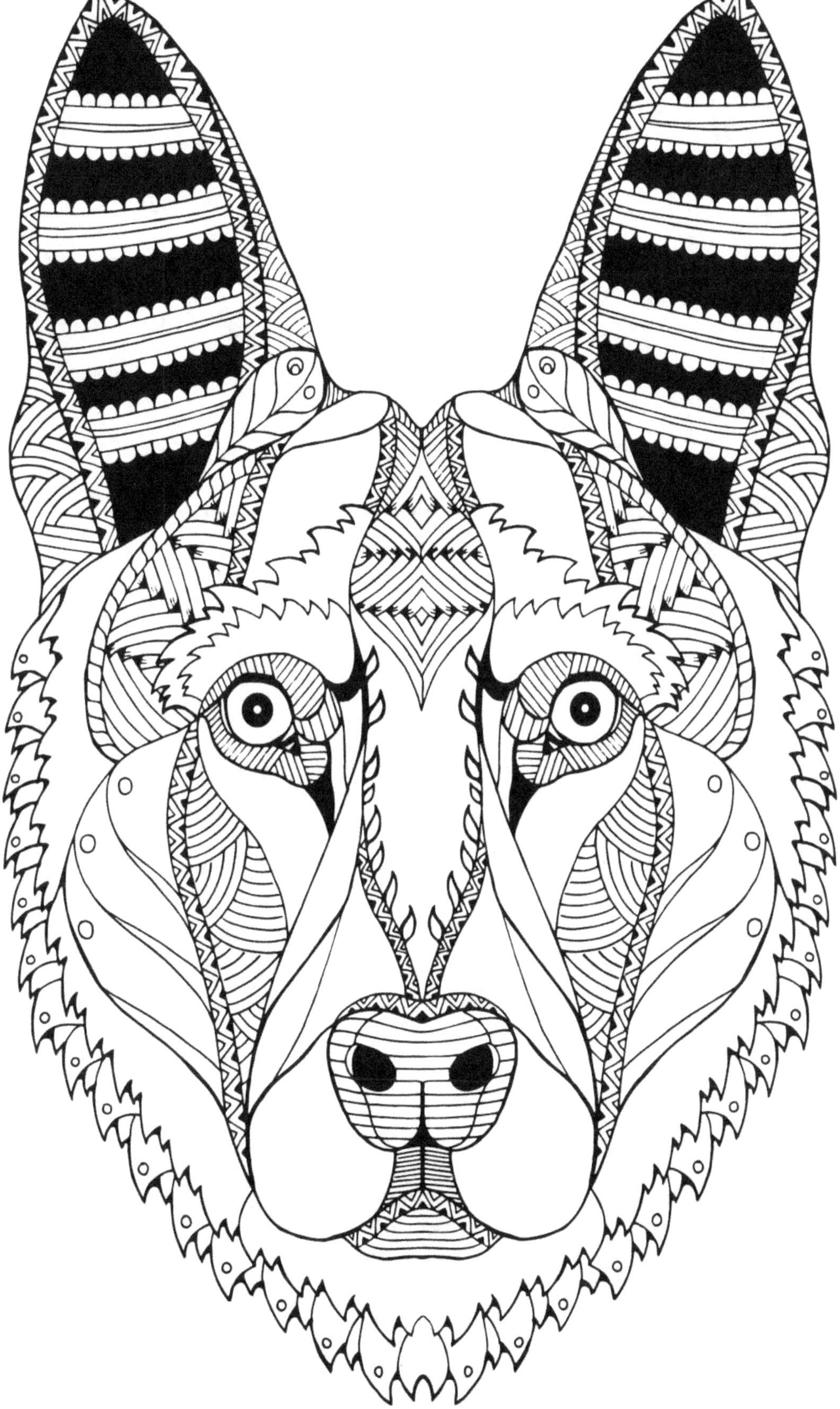

www.ingramcontent.com/pod-product-compliance
Lightning Source LLC
Chambersburg PA
CBHW081251180526
45170CB00007B/2377
9781541167957